QuickBooks
FOR
DUMMIES®
PORTABLE EDITION

by Stephen L. Nelson, CPA, MBA (finance), MS (taxation)

WILEY

John Wiley & Sons, Inc.

QuickBooks® For Dummies® Portable Edition

Published by
John Wiley & Sons, Inc.
111 River Street
Hoboken, NJ 07030-5774
www.wiley.com

Copyright © 2012 by John Wiley & Sons, Inc., Hoboken, New Jersey

Published by John Wiley & Sons, Inc., Hoboken, New Jersey

Published simultaneously in Canada

No part of this publication may be reproduced, stored in a retrieval system or transmitted in any form or by any means, electronic, mechanical, photocopying, recording, scanning or otherwise, except as permitted under Sections 107 or 108 of the 1976 United States Copyright Act, without either the prior written permission of the Publisher, or authorization through payment of the appropriate per-copy fee to the Copyright Clearance Center, 222 Rosewood Drive, Danvers, MA 01923, (978) 750-8400, fax (978) 646-8600. Requests to the Publisher for permission should be addressed to the Permissions Department, John Wiley & Sons, Inc., 111 River Street, Hoboken, NJ 07030, (201) 748-6011, fax (201) 748-6008, or online at http://www.wiley.com/go/permissions.

Trademarks: Wiley, the Wiley logo, For Dummies, the Dummies Man logo, A Reference for the Rest of Us!, The Dummies Way, Dummies Daily, The Fun and Easy Way, Dummies.com, Making Everything Easier, and related trade dress are trademarks or registered trademarks of John Wiley & Sons, Inc. and/or its affiliates in the United States and other countries, and may not be used without written permission. QuickBooks is a registered trademark of the Intuit Corporation. All other trademarks are the property of their respective owners. John Wiley & Sons, Inc., is not associated with any product or vendor mentioned in this book.

LIMIT OF LIABILITY/DISCLAIMER OF WARRANTY: THE PUBLISHER AND THE AUTHOR MAKE NO REPRESENTATIONS OR WARRANTIES WITH RESPECT TO THE ACCURACY OR COMPLETENESS OF THE CONTENTS OF THIS WORK AND SPECIFICALLY DISCLAIM ALL WARRANTIES, INCLUDING WITHOUT LIMITATION WARRANTIES OF FITNESS FOR A PARTICULAR PURPOSE. NO WARRANTY MAY BE CREATED OR EXTENDED BY SALES OR PROMOTIONAL MATERIALS. THE ADVICE AND STRATEGIES CONTAINED HEREIN MAY NOT BE SUITABLE FOR EVERY SITUATION. THIS WORK IS SOLD WITH THE UNDERSTANDING THAT THE PUBLISHER IS NOT ENGAGED IN RENDERING LEGAL, ACCOUNTING, OR OTHER PROFESSIONAL SERVICES. IF PROFESSIONAL ASSISTANCE IS REQUIRED, THE SERVICES OF A COMPETENT PROFESSIONAL PERSON SHOULD BE SOUGHT. NEITHER THE PUBLISHER NOR THE AUTHOR SHALL BE LIABLE FOR DAMAGES ARISING HEREFROM. THE FACT THAT AN ORGANIZATION OR WEBSITE IS REFERRED TO IN THIS WORK AS A CITATION AND/OR A POTENTIAL SOURCE OF FURTHER INFORMATION DOES NOT MEAN THAT THE AUTHOR OR THE PUBLISHER ENDORSES THE INFORMATION THE ORGANIZATION OR WEBSITE MAY PROVIDE OR RECOMMENDATIONS IT MAY MAKE. FURTHER, READERS SHOULD BE AWARE THAT INTERNET WEBSITES LISTED IN THIS WORK MAY HAVE CHANGED OR DISAPPEARED BETWEEN WHEN THIS WORK WAS WRITTEN AND WHEN IT IS READ.

For general information on our other products and services, please contact our Customer Care Department within the U.S. at 877-762-2974, outside the U.S. at 317-572-3993, or fax 317-572-4002.

For technical support, please visit www.wiley.com/techsupport.

Wiley also publishes its books in a variety of electronic formats and by print-on-demand. Not all content that is available in standard print versions of this book may appear or be packaged in all book formats. If you have purchased a version of this book that did not include media that is referenced by or accompanies a standard print version, you may request this media by visiting http://booksupport.wiley.com. For more information about Wiley products, visit www.wiley.com.

ISBN: 978-1-118-31518-7

Manufactured in the United States of America

10 9 8 7 6 5 4 3 2 1

WILEY

About the Author

Stephen L. Nelson, CPA, MBA (finance), MS (taxation), has a simple purpose in life: He wants to help you (and people like you) manage your business finances by using computers. Oh, sure, this personal mandate won't win him a Nobel prize or anything, but it's his own little contribution to the world.

Steve's experiences mesh nicely with his special purpose. A CPA in Redmond, Washington, his past small business experience includes a stint as an adjunct professor of taxation (S corporations and limited liability companies) at Golden Gate University graduate tax school and a few years working as a senior consultant and CPA with Arthur Andersen & Co. (er, yeah, *that* Arthur Andersen — but, hey, it was nearly 30 years ago). Steve, whose books have sold more than 4 million copies in English and have been translated into 11 other languages, is also the bestselling author of *Quicken 2012 For Dummies*

Dedication

To the entrepreneurs and small business people of the world. You folks create most of the new jobs.

Author's Acknowledgments

Hey, reader, lots of folks spent lots of time working on this book to make QuickBooks easier for you. You should know who these people are. You may just possibly meet one of them someday at a produce shop, squeezing cantaloupe, eating grapes, and looking for the perfect peach.

First, a huge thanks to the wonderful folks at Intuit who helped me by providing the beta software and other friendly assistance for this and past editions of this book.

Another big thank-you goes to the editorial folks at John Wiley & Sons, Inc., including Kevin Kirschner (project editor), Teresa Artman (copy editor), and Bob Woerner (executive editor). Thanks also to David Ringstrom for his technical assistance and superb attention to detail. Finally, thanks, too, to the composition staff.

Publisher's Acknowledgments

We're proud of this book; please send us your comments at `http://dummies.custhelp.com`. For other comments, please contact our Customer Care Department within the U.S. at 877-762-2974, outside the U.S. at 317-572-3993, or fax 317-572-4002.

Some of the people who helped bring this book to market include the following:

Acquisitions, Editorial

Project Editor: Kevin Kirschner

Executive Editor: Bob Woerner

Copy Editor: Teresa Artman

Technical Editor: David H. Ringstrom

Editorial Assistant: Amanda Graham

Sr. Editorial Assistant: Cherie Case

Cartoons: Rich Tennant
(`www.the5thwave.com`)

Composition Services

Project Coordinator: Kristie Rees

Layout and Graphics: Carrie A. Cesavice, Melanee Habig, Joyce Haughey, Lavonne Roberts

Proofreaders: Debbye Butler, Susan Moritz

Indexer: Potomac Indexing, LLC

Publishing and Editorial for Technology Dummies

> **Richard Swadley,** Vice President and Executive Group Publisher

> **Andy Cummings,** Vice President and Publisher

> **Mary Bednarek,** Executive Acquisitions Director

> **Mary C. Corder,** Editorial Director

Publishing for Consumer Dummies

> **Kathleen Nebenhaus,** Vice President and Executive Publisher

Composition Services

> **Debbie Stailey,** Director of Composition Services

Contents at a Glance

Introduction *1*

Chapter 1: Getting Started 5
Chapter 2: Populating QuickBooks Lists 27
Chapter 3: Creating Invoices and Credit Memos 75
Chapter 4: Reeling In the Dough 103
Chapter 5: Paying the Bills 131
Chapter 6: Reporting on the State of Affairs 157
Chapter 7: (Almost) Ten Tips for Business Owners 173

Index *179*

Contents

Introduction **1**

About QuickBooks 1
About This Book 2
What You Can Safely Ignore 3
What You Should Not Ignore.. 4
Three Foolish Assumptions.. 4

Chapter 1: Getting Started **5**

Why QuickBooks? 5
Getting Ready for the QuickBooks Setup 9
Stepping through the QuickBooks Setup 15
The Rest of the Story... 24

Chapter 2: Populating QuickBooks Lists **27**

The Magic and Mystery of Items.................................. 27
Adding Employees to Your Employee List 42
Customers Are Your Business....................................... 45
It's Just a Job 48
Adding Vendors to Your Vendor List............................ 52
The Other Lists... 57
Organizing Lists.. 63
Printing Lists.. 64
Exporting List Items to Your Word Processor 64
Dealing with the Chart of Accounts List 65

Chapter 3: Creating Invoices and Credit Memos **75**

Making Sure That You're Ready to Invoice Customers 75
Preparing an Invoice... 76
Fixing Invoice Mistakes 84
Preparing a Credit Memo... 86
Fixing Credit Memo Mistakes 90
History Lessons... 90
Printing Invoices and Credit Memos 91
Sending Invoices and Credit Memos via E-Mail 99
Customizing Your Invoices and Credit Memos................ 100

Chapter 4: Reeling In the Dough **103**

Recording a Sales Receipt 104
Printing a Sales Receipt 109
Special Tips for Retailers 111
Correcting Sales Receipt Mistakes 113
Recording Customer Payments 114
Correcting Mistakes in Customer Payments Entries 119
Making Bank Deposits 119
Improving Your Cash Inflow 123

Chapter 5: Paying the Bills **131**

Pay Now or Pay Later? 131
Recording Your Bills by Writing Checks 132
Recording Your Bills the Accounts Payable Way 141
Paying Your Bills 150
Tracking Vehicle Mileage 154
Paying Sales Tax 155

Chapter 6: Reporting on the State of Affairs **157**

What Kinds of Reports Are There, Anyway? 157
Creating and Printing a Report 161
Reports Made to Order 168
Processing Multiple Reports 170
Your Other Reporting Options 170
Last but Not Least: The QuickReport 171

Chapter 7: (Almost) Ten Tips for Business Owners **173**

Sign All Your Own Checks 173
Don't Sign a Check the Wrong Way 174
Review Canceled Checks Before Your Bookkeeper Does 174
Choose a Bookkeeper Who Is Familiar with Computers
     and Knows How to Do Payroll 175
Regularly Review Your Financial Statements 175
Choose an Appropriate Accounting System 176
If QuickBooks Doesn't Work for Your Business 177
Keep Things Simple 178

Index *179*

Introduction

● ●

*R*unning or working in a small business is one of the coolest things a person can do. Really. I mean it. Sure, sometimes the environment is dangerous — kind of like the Old West — but it's an environment in which you have the opportunity to make tons of money. And it's also an environment in which you can build a company or a job that fits you. In comparison, many brothers and sisters working in big-company corporate America are furiously trying to fit their round pegs into painfully square holes. Yuck.

You're wondering, of course, what any of this has to do with this book or with QuickBooks. Quite a lot, actually. The whole purpose of this book is to make it easier for you to run or work in a small business by using QuickBooks.

About QuickBooks

Let me start off with a minor but useful point: QuickBooks comes in several different flavors, including QuickBooks Basic, QuickBooks Pro, QuickBooks Premier, QuickBooks Premier Accountants Edition, and QuickBooks Enterprise Solutions.

To write this book, I used the Enterprise Solutions of QuickBooks, which is nearly identical in appearance and operation to QuickBooks Premier and QuickBooks Premier Accountants Edition.

Does this mean that I somehow leave you adrift if you have one of the other flavors? No way. I wouldn't do that to you. QuickBooks Enterprise Solutions (as well as the two Premier flavors of QuickBooks) is a superset of QuickBooks Simple Start and QuickBooks Pro. By describing how you use QuickBooks Enterprise Solutions, I also tell you how to use the other flavors of QuickBooks.

What's more, for the readers of this book, there's no discernible difference between QuickBooks Enterprise Solutions, QuickBooks Premier, and QuickBooks Pro. You aren't reading this book to prepare for the CPA exam, right? Right. The extra whistles and bells that differentiate QuickBooks Enterprise Solutions and QuickBooks Premier from QuickBooks Simple Start and QuickBooks Pro are all things that only accountants care about: remote access to QuickBooks and your QuickBooks data, reversal of general entries, extra security for general ledger closings, and so on. So I don't talk much about those things.

The bottom line? Yes, there are several flavors of QuickBooks, but if you're just trying to get started and want to use QuickBooks, this book works for QuickBooks Pro, QuickBooks Premier, and QuickBooks Enterprise Solutions.

About This Book

This book isn't meant to be read from cover to cover, like some *Stieg Larsson* page-turner. Instead, it's organized into tiny, no-sweat descriptions of how you do the things you need to do. If you're the sort of person who just doesn't feel right not reading a book from cover to cover, you can (of course) go ahead and read this thing from front to back.

I don't think this from-start-to-finish approach is bad because I tell you a bunch of stuff (tips and tricks, for example) along the way. I tried to write the book in such a way that the experience isn't as rough as you might think, and I really do think you get good value from your reading.

But you also can use this book the way you'd use an encyclopedia. If you want to know about a subject, you can look it up in the Table of Contents or the index; then you can flip to the correct chapter or page and read as much as you need or enjoy. No muss, no fuss.

I should, however, mention one thing: Accounting software programs require you to do a certain amount of preparation before you can use them to get real work done. If you haven't started to use QuickBooks yet, I recommend that you read through the first few chapters of this book to find out what you need to do first.

Hey. There's something else I should tell you. I fiddled a bit with the Windows display settings. For example, I noodled around with the font settings and most of the colors. The benefit is that the pictures in this book are easy to read. And that's good. But the cost of all this is that my pictures look a little bit different from what you see on your screen. And that's not good. In the end, however, what the publisher found is that people are happier with increased readability. Anyway, I just thought I should mention it here, upfront, in case you have any questions about it.

What You Can Safely Ignore

Sometimes I provide step-by-step descriptions of tasks. I feel very bad about having to do this, so to make things easier for you, I describe the tasks by using bold text. That way, you know exactly what you're supposed to do. I also provide a more detailed explanation in the text that follows the step. You can skip the text that accompanies the step-by-step bold-face directions if you already understand the process.

Here's an example that shows what I mean:

1. **Press Enter.**

   Find the key that's labeled Enter. Extend your index finger so that it rests ever so gently on the Enter key. In one sure, fluid motion, press the Enter key with your index finger. Then remove your finger from the key.

Okay, that example is extreme. I never go into that much detail, but you get the idea. If you know how to press Enter, you can just do that and not read further. If you need help — maybe with the finger part or something else — just read the nitty-gritty details.

Can you skip anything else? Let me see now. . . . You can skip the Technical Stuff icons, too. The information next to these icons is intended only for those of you who like that kind of technical stuff.

For that matter, I guess that you can safely ignore the stuff next to the Tip icons, too — even if the accumulated wisdom, gleaned from long hours slaving over a hot keyboard, can save you much weeping and gnashing of teeth. If you're someone who enjoys trying to do something another way, go ahead and read the tips.

Sometimes, I use made-up examples (along with examples from my own experience) to help you understand how some topic or area of QuickBooks helps you and your business, and I mark these examples with the Case Study icon. This is just my way of continuing the giving. But sure, you can skip them.

What You Should Not Ignore (Unless You're a Masochist)

Don't skip the Warning icons. They're the ones flagged with the picture of a 19th Century bomb. They describe some things that you *really* shouldn't do.

Out of respect for you, I don't put advice like "Don't smoke!" next to these icons. I figure that you're an adult, and you can make your own lifestyle decisions. So I reserve the Warning icons for more urgent and immediate dangers — things akin to "Don't smoke while you're filling your car with gasoline."

This icon is a friendly reminder to do something. Not to be too pushy, but it's probably not a good idea to ignore these babies.

Three Foolish Assumptions

I make three assumptions about you:

- ✔ **You have a PC running Microsoft Windows.** (I took pictures of the QuickBooks windows and dialog boxes while using Windows 7, in case you're interested.)
- ✔ **You know a little bit about how to work with your computer.**
- ✔ **You have or will buy a copy of QuickBooks for each computer on which you want to run the program.**

This book works for QuickBooks 2012, although in a pinch, you can probably also use it for QuickBooks 2011 or 2013. (I have to say, however, that if you have QuickBooks 2011, you may instead want to return this book and trade it in for *QuickBooks 2011 For Dummies* by yours truly.)

Chapter 1

Getting Started

- -

In This Chapter

▶ Why you truly need a tool like QuickBooks

▶ What QuickBooks actually does

▶ Getting ready to run QuickBooks Setup

▶ Stepping through QuickBooks Setup

▶ Next steps after QuickBooks Setup

- -

I know that you're eager to get started. After all, you have a business to run. But before you can start using QuickBooks, you need to do some upfront work. Specifically, you need to prepare for the QuickBooks Setup process. And then you need to walk through the Setup steps. In this chapter, I describe how you do all this stuff.

I assume that you know how Windows works. If you don't, take the time to read Chapter 1 of your Windows user's guide or try the appropriate edition of *Windows For Dummies,* by Andy Rathbone.

Why QuickBooks?

Okay, I know you know that you need an accounting system. Somebody, maybe your accountant or spouse, has convinced you of this. And you, the team player that you are, have just accepted this conventional viewpoint as the truth.

But just between you and me, why do you *really* need QuickBooks? And what does QuickBooks do that you really, truly need done? And heck, just to be truly cynical, also ask the question "Why QuickBooks?" Why not, for example, use some other accounting software program?

Why you need an accounting system

Start with the most basic question: Why do you even need an accounting system like QuickBooks? It's a fair question, so let me supply you with the two-part answer.

The first reason is that federal law requires your business to maintain an accounting system. More specifically, Section 446 (General Rule for Methods of Accounting) of Title 26 (Internal Revenue Code) of the United States Code requires that you have the ability to compute taxable income by using some sort of common-sense accounting system that clearly reflects income.

If you decide just to blow off this requirement — after all, you got into business so that you could throw off the shackles of bureaucracy — you might get away with your omission. But if the Internal Revenue Service (IRS) examines your return and you ignored Section 446, the IRS gets to do your accounting the way *it* wants. And the IRS way means that you pay more in taxes and that you also pay taxes earlier than you would have otherwise.

Here's the second reason for maintaining an accounting system. I sort of go out on an editorial limb, but I'm going to do it anyway. My strong belief — backed by more than 25 years of business experience and close-hand observations of several hundred business clients — is that you can't successfully manage your business without a decent accounting system. Success requires accurately measuring profits or losses and reasonably estimating your financial condition.

This second reason makes sense, right? If your friend Kenneth doesn't know when he's making money, which products or services are profitable, and which customers are worth keeping (and which aren't), does he really have a chance?

I don't think he does.

To summarize, your business must have a decent accounting system, no matter how you feel about accounting and regardless of how time-consuming and expensive such a system is or becomes. The law requires you to have such an accounting system. And successful business management depends on such an accounting system.

What QuickBooks does

Go on to the next question that you and I need to discuss: What does QuickBooks do to help you maintain an accounting system that measures profits and losses and other stuff like that?

QuickBooks truly makes business accounting easy by providing windows that you use to record common business transactions. For example, QuickBooks has a window (you know, a Windows window that appears on your monitor's screen) that looks like a check. To record a check you write, you fill in the blanks of the window with bits of information, such as the date, amount, and person or business you're paying.

QuickBooks also has a handful of other windows that you use in a similar fashion. For example, QuickBooks supplies an invoice window that looks like an invoice you might use to bill a customer or client. You fill in the invoice window's blanks by recording invoice information, such as the name of the client or customer, invoice amount, and date by which you want to be paid.

And here's the neat thing about these check and invoice windows: When you record business transactions by filling in the blanks shown onscreen, you collect the information that QuickBooks needs to prepare the reports that summarize your profits or losses and your financial situation.

For example, if you record two invoices (for $10,000 each) to show amounts that you billed your customers and then you record three checks (for $4,000 each) to record your advertising, rent, and supplies expenses, QuickBooks can (with two or three mouse clicks from you) prepare a report that shows your profit, as shown in Table 1-1.

Table 1-1	A Profit and Loss Report
	Amount
Revenue	$20,000
Advertising	($4,000)
Rent	($4,000)
Supplies	($4,000)
Total Expenses	($12,000)
Profit	$8,000

The parentheses, by the way, indicate negative amounts. That's an accounting thing, but back to the real point of my little narrative.

Your accounting with QuickBooks can be just as simple as I describe in the previous paragraphs. In other words, if you record just a handful of business transactions by using the correct QuickBooks windows, you can begin to prepare reports like the one shown in Table 1-1. Such reports can be used to calculate profits or (ugh) losses for last week, last month, or last year. Such reports can also be used to calculate profits and losses for particular customers and products.

I know I'm kind of harsh in the first part of this chapter — bringing up that stuff about the IRS and business failure — but this accounting stuff is neat! Good accounting gives you a way to manage your business for profitability. And obviously, all sorts of good and wonderful things stem from operating your business profitably: a materially comfortable life for you and your employees; financial cushioning to get you through the tough patches; and profits that can be reinvested in your business, in other businesses, and in community charities.

Let me also mention a couple other darn handy things that QuickBooks (and other accounting systems, too) do for you, the overworked business owner or bookkeeper:

 ✔ **Forms:** QuickBooks produces, or prints, forms such as checks or invoices by using the information you enter into those check windows and invoice windows that I mention earlier. So that's neat. And a true timesaver. (See Chapter 3.)

> ✔ **Electronic banking and billing:** QuickBooks transmits and retrieves some financial transaction information electronically. For example, QuickBooks can e-mail your invoices to customers and clients. (That can save you both time and money.) And QuickBooks can share bank accounting information with most major banks, making it easy to make payments and transfer funds electronically.

Getting Ready for the QuickBooks Setup

You need to complete three tasks to get ready for QuickBooks Setup:

> ✔ Make an important decision about your *conversion date* (the date you convert from your old accounting system to QuickBooks).

> ✔ Prepare a trial balance as of the conversion date.

> ✔ Go on a scavenger hunt to collect a bunch of stuff that you'll need or find handy for the setup.

The big decision

Before you fiddle with your computer or the QuickBooks software, you need to choose the date — the so-called *conversion date* — on which you want to begin using QuickBooks for your financial record keeping.

This decision is hugely important because the conversion date that you choose dramatically affects both the work you have to do to get QuickBooks running smoothly and the initial usefulness of the financial information that you collect and record by using QuickBooks.

You have three basic choices:

> ✔ **The right way:** You can convert at the beginning of your accounting year (which is, in most cases, the same as the beginning of the calendar year). This way is the right way for two reasons. First, converting at the beginning of the

year requires the least amount of work from you. Second, it means that you have all the current year's financial information in one system.

- ✔ **The slightly awkward way:** You can convert at the beginning of some interim accounting period (probably the beginning of some month or quarter). This approach works, but it's slightly awkward because you have to plug your year-to-date income and expenses numbers from the old system into the new system.

- ✔ **The my-way-or-the-highway way:** You can convert at some time other than what I call the right way and the slightly awkward way. Specifically, you can choose to convert whenever you jolly well feel like it. You create a bunch of unnecessary work for yourself if you take this approach, and you pull out a bunch of your hair in the process. But you also have the satisfaction of knowing that through it all, you did it your way — without any help from me.

I recommend choosing the right way. What this choice means is that if it's late in the year — say, October — you just wait until January 1 of the next year to convert. If it's still early in the year, you can also retroactively convert as of the beginning of the year. (If you do this, you need to go back and do your financial record keeping for the first part of the current year by using QuickBooks: entering sales, recording purchases, and so on.)

If it's sometime in the middle of the year — say, Memorial Day or later — you probably want to use the slightly awkward way. (I'm actually going to use the slightly awkward way in this chapter because if you see how to convert to QuickBooks by using the slightly awkward way, you know how to use both the right way and the slightly awkward way.)

The trial balance of the century

After you decide when you want to convert, you need a trial balance.

"Yikes," you say. "What's a trial balance?" A *trial balance* simply lists all your assets, liabilities, and owner's equity account balances as well as the year-to-date income and expense numbers on a specified date (which, not coincidentally, happens to be the conversion date). You need this data for the QuickBooks Setup process and for some fiddling around that you need to do after you complete the QuickBooks Setup process.

Creating a trial balance doesn't have to be as hard as it sounds. If you've been using another small business accounting system, such as the simpler Quicken product from Intuit or the Simply Accounting program from Computer Associates, you may be able to have your old system produce a trial balance on the conversion date. In that case, you can get the balances from your old system. (Consider yourself lucky if this is the case.)

Just to split hairs, the trial balance should show account balances at the very start of the first day that you'll begin using QuickBooks for actual accounting. For example, if the conversion date is 1/1/2012, the trial balance needs to show the account balances at one minute past midnight on 1/1/2012. This is also the very same thing as showing the account balances at the very end of the last day that you'll be using the old accounting system — in other words, at exactly midnight on 12/31/2011 if you're converting to QuickBooks on 1/1/2012.

If your old system is rather informal (perhaps it's a shoebox full of receipts), or if it tracks only cash (perhaps you've been using Quicken), you need to do a bit more work:

- ✔ **To get your cash balance:** Reconcile your bank account or bank accounts (if you have more than one bank account) as of the conversion date.

- ✔ **To get your accounts receivable balance:** Tally the total of all your unpaid customer invoices.

- ✔ **To get your other asset account balances:** Know what each asset originally costs. For depreciable fixed assets, you also need to provide any accumulated depreciation that has been claimed for that asset. (*Accumulated depreciation* is the total depreciation that you've already expensed for each asset.)

- ✔ **To get your liability account balances:** Know how much you owe on each liability. If you trust your *creditors* — the people to whom you owe the money — you may also be able to get this information from their statements.

You don't need to worry about the owner's equity accounts. QuickBooks can calculate your owner's equity account balances for you, based on the difference between your total assets and your total liabilities. This method is a bit sloppy, and accountants may not like it, but it's a pretty good compromise. (If you do have detailed account balances for your owner's equity accounts, use these figures — and know that you're one in a million.)

If you're using the slightly awkward way to convert to QuickBooks — in other words, if your conversion date is some date other than the beginning of the accounting year — you also need to provide year-to-date income and expense balances. To get your income, cost of goods sold, expenses, other income, and other expense account balances, you need to calculate the year-to-date amount of each account. If you can get this information from your old system, that's super. If not, you need to get it manually. (If you suddenly have images of yourself sitting at your desk late at night, tapping away on a ten-key, you're probably right. What's more, you probably also need to allocate half of another Saturday to getting QuickBooks up and running.)

Just for fun, I created the sample trial balance shown in Table 1-2. This table shows you what a trial balance looks like if you convert at some time other than at the beginning of the accounting year.

Table 1-2	A "Slightly Awkward Way" Sample Trial Balance	
Trial Balance Information	*Debit*	*Credit*
Assets		
Checking	$5,000	
Fixed assets	$60,000	
Accumulated depreciation (fixed assets)		$2,000
Liabilities information		
Loan payable		$10,000
Owner's equity and income statement information		
Opening bal equity		$20,000

Trial Balance Information	Debit	Credit
Sales		$60,000
Cost of goods sold	$20,000	
Supplies expense	$2,100	
Rent expense	$4,900	
Totals	**$92,000**	**$92,000**

If you're converting at the very beginning of the accounting year, your trial balance instead looks like the one shown in Table 1-3. Notice that this trial balance doesn't have any year-to-date income or expense balances.

Table 1-3   A "Right Way" Sample Trial Balance

Trial Balance Information	Debit	Credit
Assets		
Checking	$5,000	
Fixed assets	$60,000	
Accumulated depreciation (fixed assets)		$2,000
Liabilities information		
Loan payable		$10,000
Owner's equity and income statement information		
Opening bal equity		$53,000
Totals	**$65,000**	**$65,000**

The mother of all scavenger hunts

Even after you decide when you want to convert to QuickBooks and you come up with a trial balance, you still need to collect a bunch of additional information. I list these items in laundry-list fashion. What you want to do is find all this stuff and then pile it up (neatly) in a big stack next to the computer:

✔ **Last year's federal tax return:** QuickBooks asks which
federal income tax form you use to file your tax return
and also about your Taxpayer Identification number. Last
year's federal tax return is the easiest place to find this
stuff.

✔ **Copies of all your most recent state and federal payroll tax returns:** If you prepare payroll for employees,
QuickBooks wants to know about the federal and state
payroll tax rates that you pay, as well as some other
stuff.

✔ **Copies of all the unpaid invoices that your customers
(or clients or patients or whatever) owe you as of the
conversion date:** I guess this is probably obvious, but
the total accounts receivable balance shown on your trial
balance needs to match the total of the unpaid customer
invoices.

✔ **Copies of all unpaid bills that you owe your vendors
as of the conversion date:** Again, this is probably obvious, but the total accounts payable balance shown on
your trial balance needs to match the total of the unpaid
vendor bills.

✔ **A detailed listing of any inventory items you're holding
for resale:** This list should include not only inventory
item descriptions and quantities, but also the initial purchase prices and the anticipated sales prices. In other
words, if you sell porcelain wombats and you have 1,200
of these beauties in inventory, you need to know exactly
what you paid for them.

✔ **Copies of the prior year's W-2 statements, W-4 statements for anybody you hired since the beginning of
the prior year, detailed information about any payroll
tax liabilities you owe as of the conversion date, and
detailed information about the payroll tax deposits
you made since the beginning of the year:** You need
the information shown on these forms to adequately and
accurately set up the QuickBooks payroll feature. I don't
want to scare you, but this is probably the most tedious
part of setting up QuickBooks.

✔ **If you're retroactively converting as of the beginning
of the year, you need a list of all the transactions that
have occurred since the beginning of the year:** sales,

purchases, payroll transactions, and everything and anything else: If you do the right-way conversion retro-actively, you need to re-enter each of these transactions into the new system. You actually enter the information after you complete the QuickBooks Setup that I describe later in this chapter, but you might as well get all this information together now, while you're searching for the rest of the items for this scavenger hunt.

If you take the slightly awkward way, you don't need to find the last item that I describe in the preceding list. You can just use the year-to-date income and expense numbers from the trial balance.

Stepping through the QuickBooks Setup

After you decide when you want to convert, prepare a trial balance as of the conversion date, and collect the additional raw data that you need, you're ready to step through the QuickBooks Setup. You'll need to start QuickBooks and then walk through the steps.

Starting QuickBooks

To start QuickBooks 2012, click the Windows Start button and then click the menu choice that leads to QuickBooks. (For example, I choose Start⇨All Programs⇨QuickBooks⇨ QuickBooks Enterprise Solutions 12.) Or double-click the QuickBooks program icon if you put one on the desktop during the installation.

QuickBooks comes in several flavors. The most common flavors are QuickBooks Simple Start, QuickBooks Pro, QuickBooks Premier, and QuickBooks Enterprise Solutions. These four programs differ in several significant ways: QuickBooks Simple Start is a special "light" version of QuickBooks, which looks completely different. (I wrote another book, *QuickBooks Simple Start For Dummies*, which you should use instead of this book if you're working with QuickBooks Simple Start.) QuickBooks Pro includes the advanced job costing and time-estimating features; it also includes the capability to share a QuickBooks file over a network. QuickBooks Premier has features beyond the QuickBooks Pro features for accountants and auditors who want to use QuickBooks for rather large small businesses. Finally, QuickBooks Enterprise Solutions is nearly identical to QuickBooks Premier but allows for very large QuickBooks files, including much larger customer, vendor, and employee lists.

I used the Accountants Edition of QuickBooks Enterprise Solutions, so some of the figures might differ a wee bit from what you see onscreen. The Accountants Edition allows me to pretend I'm using pretty much any version of QuickBooks, so I opted for QuickBooks Enterprise Solutions. Aside from minor cosmetic differences, the various versions of QuickBooks all work the same way. You can use this book for any of these program versions.

If this is the first time you started QuickBooks, QuickBooks displays the QuickBooks Setup window with the message, `Let's get your business set up quickly!` (see Figure 1-1).

Figure 1-1: The first QuickBooks Setup window.

If you've already been using an earlier version of QuickBooks, QuickBooks should prompt you to open (and possibly convert) an existing file — and you don't need to be reading this chapter.

If you aren't starting QuickBooks for the first time but you want to step through the QuickBooks Setup to set up a new company anyway, choose File⇨New Company.

I should mention that the first QuickBooks Setup dialog box identifies some other setup options you can use to get started. For example, the dialog box gives you the option of an Advanced Setup, which sounds a little scary. And the dialog box also suggests that you might want to upgrade from Quicken or some other accounting system. (Basically, that upgrade just means that you want QuickBooks to try using your existing accounting system's data as a starting point for QuickBooks.)

Two simple bits of advice: Don't fiddle with the Advanced Setup unless you're an accounting expert. And don't attempt to "upgrade" Quicken or some other accounting program's data. It's just as easy and usually considerably cleaner to work from a trial balance.

The one group of new QuickBooks users who should probably try upgrading their old accounting system's data are people who've done a really good job of keeping their books with the old system, including complete balance sheet information. No offense, but you probably aren't in this category. Sorry.

Using the Express Setup

QuickBooks 2012 provides a much accelerated (and surprisingly good!) setup process compared with past versions of the software. Basically, you'll fill in some boxes and click some buttons, and, *voilà,* you find that you've largely set up QuickBooks. Because I can give you some tips, identify some shortcuts, and warn you of some traps you want to avoid, I'm going to provide step-by-step instructions.

1. **Choose to use the Express Setup.**

   With the first QuickBooks Setup dialog box displayed (refer to Figure 1-1), click the Express Start button. QuickBooks displays the Tell Us about Your Business dialog box. See Figure 1-2.

Intuit QuickBooks Enterprise Solutions: Accountant 12.0

File Edit View Lists Favorites Accountant Company Customers Vendors Employees Banking Reports Online Solutions Window Help Beta

QuickBooks Setup

Tell us about your business

Enter the essentials so we can create a company file that's just right for your business.

| * Company Name | Pine Lake Porcelain, LLC |
| | We'll use this on your invoices and reports, and to name your company file. |

| * Industry | Retail Shop or Online Commerce | Help me choose |
| | We'll use this to create accounts common for your industry. |

| * Company Type | Single-Member LLC (Form-1040) ▼ | Help me choose |
| | We'll use this to select the right tax settings for your business. |

| Tax ID # | 123456789 | ❓ |
| | We'll use this on your tax forms. |

* Require

📖 Need help? Give us a call   Back   Continue

Figure 1-2: The Tell Us about Your Business dialog box.

2. Specify the business name.

The name you specify goes on QuickBooks reports and appears on invoices you send customers. Accordingly, you want to use your "real" business name. And if your business is incorporated or formed as a limited liability company (LLC), you want to use the right suffix or acronym in your name. For example, don't use *Acme Supplies* but rather *Acme Supplies Incorporated* or *Acme Supplies LLC.*

Note: QuickBooks also uses the company name for the QuickBooks data file.

3. Identify your industry.

For example, if you're in the construction business, type **construction.** When you type something into the Industry field, QuickBooks turns the box into a drop-down list showing the industries that it recognizes. You can pick an industry from this list (or pick the industry that's closest to your business).

Be thoughtful and cautious about the industry you specify. QuickBooks sets up a starting chart of accounts for you based on the industry. A chart of accounts lists the asset, liability, income, and expense accounts (or categories) that QuickBooks will use to categorize your business's finances.

4. Identify the tax return you file and your taxpayer identification number.

Use the Company Type field to specify the tax return that your business files. You can click in that field and then select from the list that QuickBooks provides.

Use the Tax ID # field to provide your business taxpayer identification number. If you're a sole proprietorship without employees, your tax identification number may be your Social Security number. In all other cases, your taxpayer identification number is your Employer Identification number.

5. Click the Continue button.

6. On the next page, supply your business contact information.

When QuickBooks displays the Enter Your Business Contact Information dialog box (see Figure 1-3), verify that the correct business name shows in the Legal Name field. Then fill in the rest of the address and contact information. I hope you don't feel cheated that I'm not giving you instructions like "Enter your street address into the Address box" and "Please remember that your telephone number goes into the Phone box."

If you ever decide that you want to change some piece of information that you entered on a previous page of the QuickBooks Setup dialog box, you can just click the Back button to back up.

If you're an observant person, you may have noticed the Preview Your Settings button that appears on the Enter Your Business Contact Information dialog box. You can safely ignore this button, but if you're a truly curious cat, go ahead and click the button. QuickBooks will then display a dialog box that identifies which standard QuickBooks features the QuickBooks Setup process is turning on and which asset, liability, income, and expense accounts will initially appear on your chart of accounts. Oh, one other thing: The Preview Your Company Settings dialog box also provides a Company File Location tab that identifies where your QuickBooks data file will be located.

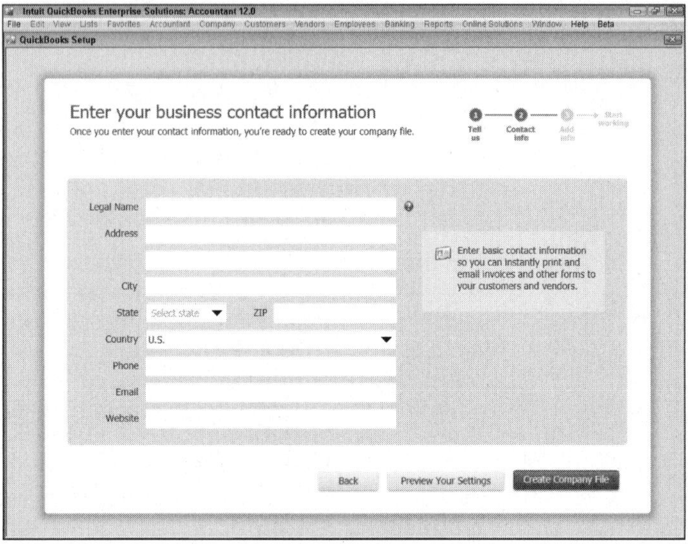

Figure 1-3: The Enter Your Business Contact Information dialog box.

7. **Create the QuickBooks data file.**

   After you provide the business contact information requested by QuickBooks, click the Create Company File button. QuickBooks creates the data file it will use to store your financial information. (In some versions of QuickBooks, the file creation process takes a few minutes.) When QuickBooks finishes creating your file, it displays the You've Got a Company File! dialog box (see Figure 1-4).

8. **Identify your customers, vendors, and employees.**

   With the You've Got a Company File! dialog box displayed, click the Add the People You Do Business With button. QuickBooks displays another dialog box that asks, "Perchance, are contact names and addresses stored electronically someplace else like Microsoft Outlook or Google Gmail?"

   - *If you do have contact name and address information stored someplace else that QuickBooks will retrieve:* Click the appropriate button and follow the onscreen instructions.

   - *Otherwise:* Click the Paste from Excel or Enter Manually button and then Continue.

Figure 1-4: The You've Got a Company File! dialog box.

When QuickBooks displays the Add the People You Do Business With dialog box (see Figure 1-5), use the rows of the displayed worksheet to describe your customers, vendors, and employees. To enter a contact into the next empty row

a. *Select the Customer, Vendor, or Employee radio button (as appropriate).*

b. *Describe the contact using the fields provided: Name, Company Name, First Name, Last Name, Email, Phone, and so forth.* Each contact goes into its own row.

c. *Click the Continue button twice when you finish identifying your contacts to return to the You've Got a Company File! dialog box.*

In the first Name column, which is used for customers and vendors, provide a short abbreviated name or nickname for a contact. You'll use what you specify in the Name column within QuickBooks to refer to the contact, so you want to use something short and sweet. For example, if you're working with, say, customer John Smith at IBM Corporation, you might enter **IBM** into the Name column, **IBM Corporation** into the

Company Name column, **John** into the First Name column, and so forth.

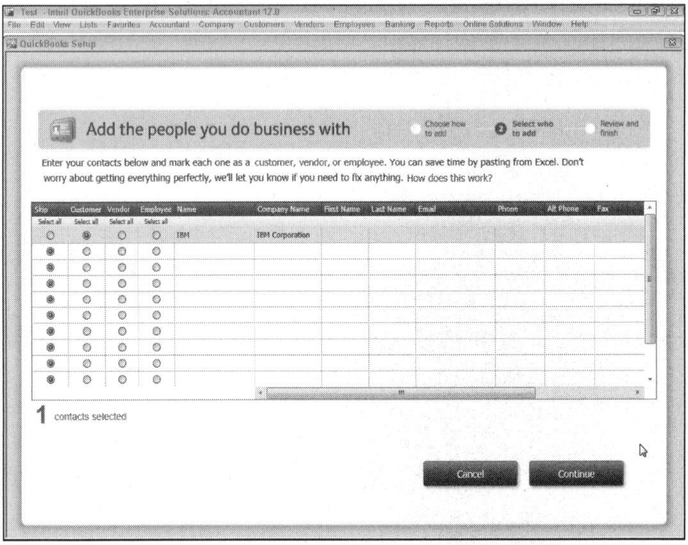

Figure 1-5: The Add the People You Do Business With dialog box.

If you add any customers or vendors, QuickBooks asks about open balances that customers owe you or that you owe vendors after you click the Continue button to leave the Add the People You Do Business With dialog box. You don't need to worry about these open balances at this point of the QuickBooks Setup process. I describe how to cleanly and correctly deal with open customer and vendor balances in Chapter 4.

9. Identify the items (the stuff) you sell.

With the You've Got a Company File! dialog box displayed, click the Add the Products and Services You Sell button. QuickBooks displays another dialog box that asks what kind of stuff you want to describe: services, stuff that you track in inventory, stuff that is inventory but that you don't track, and so on. (Which items QuickBooks lists depends on the industry that you specify in Step 3.) Click the appropriate button.

When QuickBooks displays the Add the Products and Services You Sell dialog box (see Figure 1-6), use the rows of the displayed worksheet to describe product or service. For any item, you'll always enter a name, description, and price. For some items, however, you can specify much greater detail than just this skeletal information. Click the Continue button when you finish identifying your products and services to return to the You've Got a Company File! dialog box.

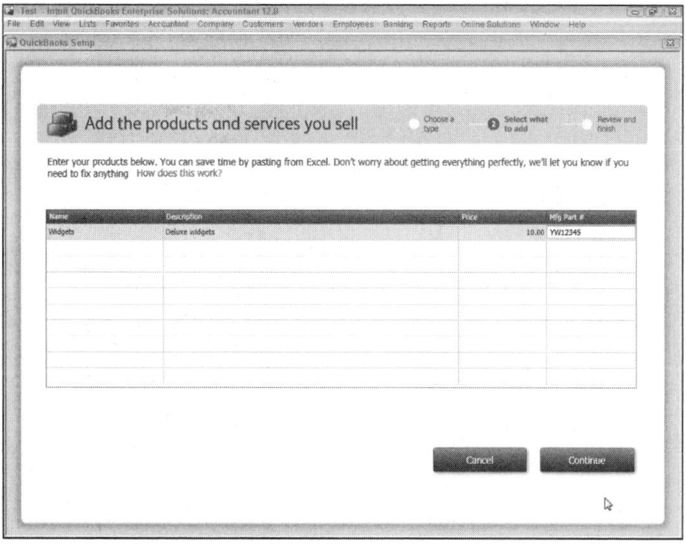

Figure 1-6: The Add the Products and Services You Sell dialog box.

10. Describe your bank account(s).

With the You've Got a Company File! dialog box displayed, click the Add Your Bank Accounts button. When QuickBooks displays the Add Your Bank Accounts dialog box (see Figure 1-7), use the worksheet to describe each bank account of your business: its name, account number, balance at the conversion date, and the actual conversion date. Click the Continue button when you finish identifying your products and services to return to the You've Got a Company File! dialog box.

11. Start working with QuickBooks.

With the You've Got a Company File dialog box displayed, click the Start Working button. QuickBooks displays the QuickBooks program window. You're done.

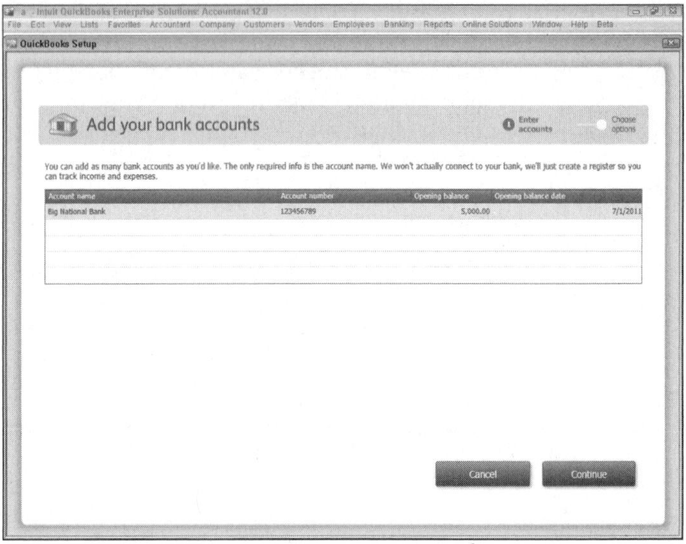

Figure 1-7: The Add Your Bank Accounts dialog box.

At some point after QuickBooks starts, you will see a message box that asks whether you want to register QuickBooks. If you don't register, you can use the product roughly a few times, and then — whammo! The program locks up, and you can no longer access your files. Either you register it, or you can't use it. I don't like being forced to do something, but getting worked up about having to register QuickBooks is a waste of time.

The simplest option is to just register. Here's how: When QuickBooks displays the message box that asks whether you want to register, click the Online button to register online, or click the Phone button to register over the phone. If you go with the Phone option, QuickBooks displays another dialog box that gives you a telephone number to call and provides a space for you to enter your registration number.

The Rest of the Story

Throughout the preceding paragraphs in this chapter, I describe how you prepare for and then step through the QuickBooks Setup process. When the QuickBooks Setup is over, though, you need to take care of three other little jobs:

✔ You need to describe in detail your inventory, your customer receivables, and (if you chose to track vendor bills
you owe) your vendor payables.

✔ You need to describe your current business finances,
including any year-to-date revenue and year-to-date
expenses that aren't recorded as part of getting your
customer receivables and vendor payables entered into
QuickBooks.

✔ If you want to use accrual-basis accounting, you need to
make an adjustment.

These chores aren't time consuming, but they are the
three most complicated tasks that you need to do to set up
QuickBooks.

To set up the inventory records, you just identify the item
counts you hold in inventory, as described in Chapter 4.

To set up your customer receivables and (if necessary)
vendor payables, you first need to enter customer invoices
that were prepared prior to the conversion date but that are
still uncollected at conversion, as described in Chapter 4.
Similarly, you may need to enter vendor payables that were
incurred prior to the conversion date but that are still unpaid
at conversion.

I talk about this stuff more in Chapter 2, so if you're still okay
with doing some more installation and setup work, go ahead
and flip there.

Chapter 2

Populating QuickBooks Lists

· ·

In This Chapter

▶ Adding items to the Item list

▶ Adding employees to the Employee list

▶ Adding new customers and jobs

▶ Adding new vendors

▶ Understanding and using the other lists

▶ Organizing, printing, and exporting lists

▶ Dealing with the Chart of Accounts list

· ·

*T*he QuickBooks Setup (which I discuss at some length in Chapter 1) doesn't actually get QuickBooks completely ready to use. You also need to enter additional information about your products, employees, customers, and vendors (and a handful of other items) into lists. In this chapter, I describe how you create and work with these lists. I also describe how you clean up some of the accounting messiness created when you enter information into these lists.

The Magic and Mystery of Items

The first QuickBooks list you need to finish setting up is the *Item list* — the list of stuff you buy and sell. Before you start adding to your Item list, however, I need to tell you that QuickBooks isn't very smart about its view of what you buy and sell. It thinks that anything you stick on a sales invoice or a purchase order is something you're selling.

If you sell colorful coffee mugs, for example, you probably figure (and correctly so) that you need to add descriptions of each of these items to the Item list. However, if you add freight charges to an invoice, QuickBooks thinks that you're adding another mug. And if you add sales tax to an invoice, well, guess what? QuickBooks again thinks that you're adding another mug.

This wacky definition of items is confusing at first. But just remember one thing, and you'll be okay: You aren't the one who's stupid: QuickBooks is. No, I'm not saying that QuickBooks is a bad program. It's a wonderful accounting program and a great tool. What I'm saying is that QuickBooks is only a dumb computer program; it isn't an artificial-intelligence program. It doesn't pick up on the little subtleties of business — such as the fact that even though you charge customers for freight, you aren't really in the shipping business.

Each entry on the invoice or purchase order — the mugs that you sell, the subtotal, the discount, the freight charges, and the sales tax — is an *item.* Yes, I know this setup is weird, but getting used to the wackiness now makes the discussions that follow much easier to understand.

If you want to see a sample invoice, take a peek at Figure 2-1. Just so you're not confused, to make more room for the invoice window, I removed the QuickBooks Navigation bar that typically appears along the left edge of the QuickBooks window.

Do you see those first three items: Rainbow Mugs, Yellow Mugs, and Blue Mugs? You can see the sense of calling them *items,* right? These mugs are things that you sell.

But then suppose that you give frequent buyers of your merchandise a 10 percent discount. To include this discount in your accounting, you need to add a Subtotal item to tally the sale and then a Discount item to calculate the discount. Figure 2-1 also shows this. See it? Kind of weird, eh?

Then look at the Shipping and Handling item, which charges the customer $50 for freight. Yep, that's right — another item. In sum, everything that appears on an invoice or a purchase order is an item that you need to describe in your Item list.

Just above the invoice total, if you look closely, you can see another item for including sales tax on your invoices — and that's really an item, too.

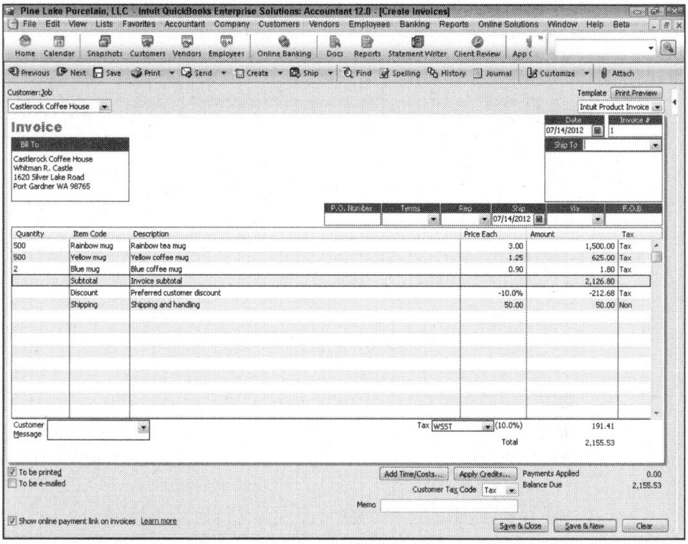

Figure 2-1: A sample QuickBooks invoice.

I describe creating invoices in Chapter 3.

Adding items you might include on invoices

You may have added some items as part of the QuickBooks Setup, but you'll want to know how to add any other needed items and how to add new items. To add invoice or purchase order items to the Item list, follow these steps:

1. Choose Lists➪Item List.

When QuickBooks asks whether you want to set up multiple items, indicate, "No way, man." QuickBooks then displays the Item List window, as shown in Figure 2-2.

When QuickBooks asks whether you want to add multiple items at one time, you can reply, "Why, yes, thank you very much." Then QuickBooks displays a worksheet like the one used during the QuickBooks Setup I describe in Chapter 1 that you can use to set up multiple items in one fell swoop.

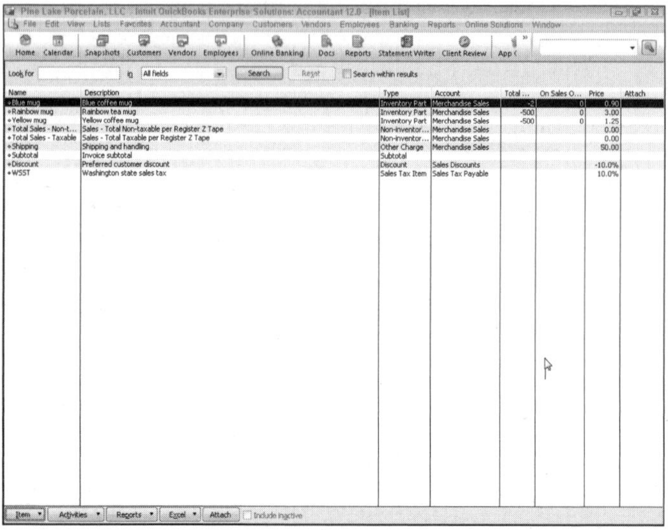

Figure 2-2: The QuickBooks Item List window.

2. **Click the Item button at the bottom of the Item List window and then choose New from the drop-down list.**

   QuickBooks displays the New Item window, as shown in Figure 2-3.

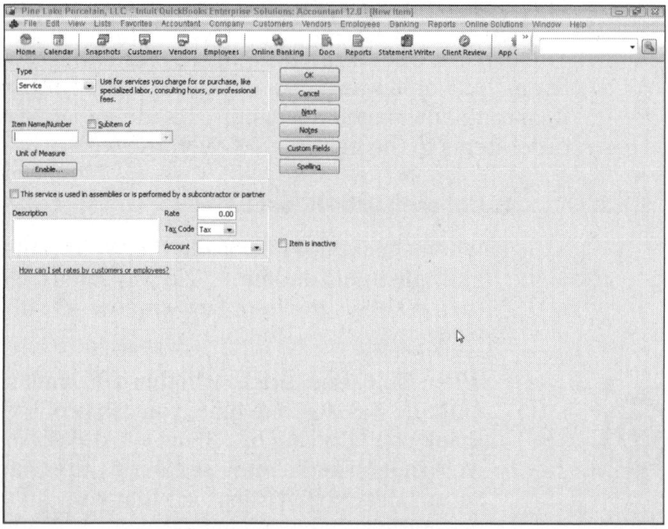

Figure 2-3: The QuickBooks New Item window.

3. **Categorize the item.**

   Select an item type from the Type drop-down list. The Item list that you see is dependent on the type of business you told QuickBooks you were in when you set up the program, so use the following as a sample — the amount and type of items that you need depend on the business you're in. Select one of the following item types by clicking the name in the list:

   - *Service:* Select this type if you charge for a service — such as an hour of labor or a repair job.

   - *Inventory Part:* Select this type if what you sell is something that you buy from someone else, and you want to track your holdings of the item. If you sell thingamajigs that you purchase from the manufacturer Thingamajigs Amalgamated, for example, you specify the item type as Inventory Part.

   - *Inventory Assembly:* Select this type if what you sell is something that you make from other Inventory items. In other words, if you buy raw materials or other components and then assemble these things to create your finished product, the finished product is an Inventory Assembly item.

   - *Non-Inventory Part:* Select this type if what you sell is something that you don't want to track as inventory. (You usually don't use this item type for products that you sell, by the way. Instead, you use it for items that you buy for the business and need to include on purchase orders.)

   - *Other Charge:* Select this item type for things such as freight and handling charges that you include on invoices.

   - *Subtotal:* This item type adds everything before you subtract any discount, add the sales tax, and so on.

   - *Group:* Use this item type to enter a bunch of items (which are already on the list) at one time. This item is a nice timesaver. For example, if you commonly sell sets of items, you don't have to specify those items individually every time you write an invoice.

- *Discount:* This item type calculates an amount to be subtracted from a subtotal.

- *Payment:* This option is wacky, but if your invoice sometimes includes an entry that reduces the invoice total — customer deposits at the time of sale, for example — select this item type. If this item type confuses you, just ignore it.

- *Sales Tax Item:* Select this item type for the sales tax that you include on the invoice.

- *Sales Tax Group:* This item type is similar to the Group item type, but you use it only for sales taxes that are collected in one transaction and owed to multiple agencies.

4. **Type an item number or name.**

   Press the Tab key or use your mouse to click the Item Name/Number text box below the Type drop-down list. Then type a short description of the item.

5. **(Optional) Make the item a subitem.**

   If you want to work with *subitems* — items that appear within other items — select the Subitem Of check box and use the corresponding drop-down list to specify the parent item to which a subitem belongs.

   If you set up a parent item for coffee mugs and sub-items for blue, yellow, and rainbow mugs, for example, you can produce reports that show parent items (such as mugs) and subitems (such as the differently colored mugs). Subitems are just an extra complexity, so if you're new to this QuickBooks stuff, I suggest that you keep things simple by avoiding them.

6. **Describe the item in more detail.**

   Move the cursor to the Description text box and type a description. This description then appears on the invoice. Note that if you specified the item type as Inventory Part in Step 3, you see two description text boxes: Description on Purchase Transactions and Description on Sales Transactions. The purchase description appears on purchase orders, and the sales description appears on sales invoices.

7. **If the item type is Service, Non-Inventory Part, or Other Charge, tell QuickBooks how much to charge for the item, whether the item is subject to sales tax, and which income account to use for tracking the income that you receive from selling the item.**

   - *For a Service type,* use the Rate text box to specify the price you charge for one unit of the service. If you charge by the hour, for example, the rate is the charge for an hour of service. If you charge for a job — such as a repair job or the completion of a specific task — the rate is the charge for the job or task.

   - *For a Non-Inventory Part type,* use the Price text box to specify the amount you charge for the item.

   - *For an Other Charge type,* use the Amount or % text box, which replaces the Rate text box, to specify the amount you charge for the item. You can type an amount, such as **20** for $20.00, or you can type a percentage. If you type a percentage, QuickBooks calculates the Other Charge Amount as the percentage multiplied by the preceding item shown on the invoice. (You usually put in an Other Charge after using a Subtotal item — something I talk about in the "Creating other wacky items for invoices" section, later in this chapter.)

   - *For all three types,* use the Tax Code drop-down list to indicate whether the item is taxed. (Note that the Tax Code field appears only if you told QuickBooks in the QuickBooks Setup that you charge customers sales tax.)

   - *For all three types,* use the Account drop-down list to specify which income account you want to use to track the income that you receive from the sale of this item.

8. **If the item type is Inventory Part, tell QuickBooks how much to charge for the inventory part, how much the inventory part costs, and which income account to use for tracking the product sales income.**

   For an Inventory Part item type, QuickBooks displays the New Item window, as shown in Figure 2-4.

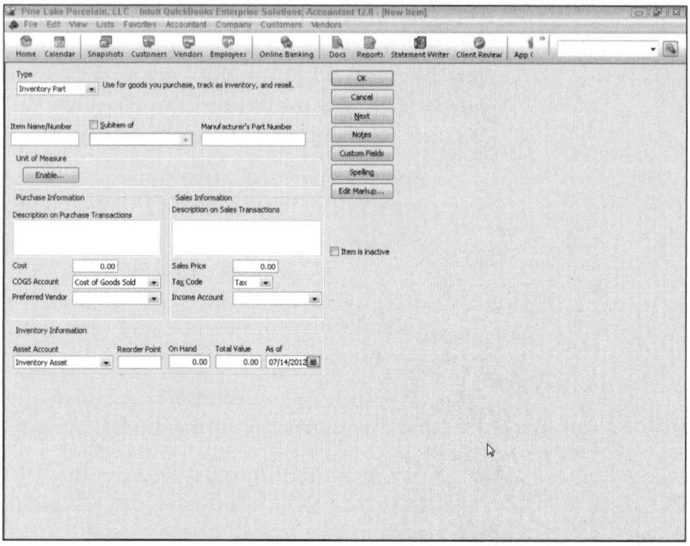

Figure 2-4: The QuickBooks New Item window with the Inventory Part item type selected.

You use the extra fields that this special version of the window displays to record the following information:

- *Description on Purchase Transactions:* Describe the part. This description appears on the documents (such as purchase orders) that you use when you buy items for your inventory.

- *Cost:* Specify the average cost per unit of the items that you currently have. This field acts as the default rate when you enter the item on a purchase transaction.

- *COGS (Cost of Goods Sold) Account:* Specify the account that you want QuickBooks to use for tracking this item's cost when you sell it. (QuickBooks suggests the Cost of Goods Sold account. If you've created other accounts for your COGS, select the appropriate account.)

- *Preferred Vendor:* Specify your first choice when ordering the item for your business. (If the vendor isn't on your Vendor list, QuickBooks asks you to add it. If you say, "Yeah, I do want to add it," QuickBooks displays the Add Vendor window, which you can then use to describe the vendor.)

- *Description on Sales Transactions:* Type a description of the item that you want to appear on documents, such as invoices and so on, that your customers see. (QuickBooks suggests the same description that you used in the Description on Purchase Transactions text box as a default.)

- *Sales Price:* Enter the amount that you charge for the item.

- *Tax Code:* Indicate whether the item is taxed.

- *Income Account:* Specify the account that you want QuickBooks to use for tracking the income from the sale of the part. This is probably the Resale Income or Sales account. You typically use the Resale Income account to track wholesale (nontaxable) sales and the Sales account to track retail (taxable) sales.

- *Asset Account:* Specify the other current asset account that you want QuickBooks to use for tracking this Inventory item's value.

- *Reorder Point:* Specify the lowest inventory quantity of this item that can remain before you order more. When the inventory level drops to this quantity, QuickBooks adds a Reminder to the Reminders list, notifying you that you need to reorder the item. (To see the Reminders list, choose Lists⇨Reminders.)

- *On Hand:* Set this field to the physical count for the item at the conversion date if you're setting up an item for the first time as part of setting up QuickBooks. Otherwise, leave this field set to zero.

- *Total Value:* Leave this field at zero, too.

- *As Of:* Enter the current date.

9. **If the item type is Inventory Assembly, tell QuickBooks which COGS and income account to use for tracking the item, how much to charge for the inventory assembly, and how to build the item from other component inventory items.**

Note: The Inventory Assembly item is available in QuickBooks Premier and Enterprise but is not in Simple Start or QuickBooks Pro.

For an Inventory Assembly item type, QuickBooks displays the New Item window.

You use the extra fields that this special version of the window displays to record the following information:

- *COGS (Cost of Goods Sold) Account:* Specify the account that you want QuickBooks to use for tracking this item's cost when you sell it. (QuickBooks suggests the Cost of Goods Sold account. If you've created other accounts for your COGS, select the appropriate account.)

- *Description:* Type a description of the item that you want to appear on documents that your customers see, such as invoices.

- *Sales Price:* Enter the amount that you charge for the item.

- *Tax Code:* Indicate whether the item is taxed.

- *Income Account:* Specify the account that you want QuickBooks to use for tracking the income from the sale of the part. This is probably the Resale Income or Sales account. You typically use the Resale Income account to track wholesale (nontaxable) sales and the Sales account to track retail (taxable) sales.

- *Bill of Materials:* Use the Bill of Materials list to identify the component items and the quantities needed to make the inventory assembly.

- *Asset Account:* Specify the other current asset account that you want QuickBooks to use for tracking this inventory item's value.

- *Build Point:* Specify the lowest inventory quantity of this item that can remain before you manufacture more. When the inventory level drops to this quantity, QuickBooks adds a Reminder to the Reminders list, notifying you that you need to make more of the item.

- *On Hand:* Set this field to the physical count for the item at the conversion date if you're setting up an item for the first time as part of setting up QuickBooks. Otherwise, leave this field set to zero.

- *Total Value:* If you enter a value other than zero into the On Hand field, set the total value amount as the cost of the items you're holding. Otherwise, leave this field at zero.

- *As Of:* Enter the conversion date into the As Of text box if you're describing some item as part of getting QuickBooks set up. Otherwise, just enter the current date.

10. If the item type is Sales Tax Item, tell QuickBooks what sales tax rate to charge and what government agency to pay.

Note: The Sales Tax Item version of the New Item window looks a little different from the window shown earlier in Figure 2-4. This is straightforward stuff, though. Enter the sales tax rate into the appropriate box and the state (or the city or other tax agency name) into the appropriate box:

- *Sales Tax Name and Description:* Specify further details for later identification.

- *Tax Rate:* Specify the sales tax rate as a percentage.

- *Tax Agency:* Name the state or local tax agency that collects all the loot that you remit. If the tax agency isn't on the list, you can add it by selecting Add New from the drop-down list.

11. If the item type is Payment, describe the payment method and how you want QuickBooks to handle the payment.

You use payment items to record a down payment made when the invoice is created to reduce the final balance due from the customer later. *Note:* Retainers and Advance Deposits are handled differently.

The Payment version of the New Item window looks a little different from the window shown in Figure 2-4.

Use the Payment Method drop-down list to specify the method of payment for a Payment. QuickBooks provides a starting list of several of the usual payment methods. You can easily add more payment types by choosing Add New from the drop-down list. When you choose this entry, QuickBooks displays the New Payment Method dialog box. In the dialog box's only text box, identify the payment method: cows, beads, shells, or some other what-have-you.

When you're finished, use the area in the lower-left corner of the New Item window to either group the payment with other undeposited funds or, if you use the drop-down list, deposit the payment to a specific account.

12. **Click OK or Next when you're finished.**

When you finish describing one item, click OK to add the item to the list and return to the Item List window. Click Next to add the item to the list and keep the New Item window onscreen so that you can add more items.

13. **If you added a new Inventory item, record the purchase of the item.**

After you finish describing any new inventory items, you need to make another transaction to categorize the purchase of the items (unless they just showed up one morning on your doorstep).

Creating other wacky items for invoices

In the preceding section, I don't describe all the items that you can add. For example, you can create a *Subtotal item* to calculate the subtotal of the items you list on an invoice. (You usually need this subtotal when you want to calculate a sales tax on the invoice's items.) You might want to create other wacky items for your invoices as well, such as discounts. I describe these special types of items in the next few sections.

Creating Subtotal items to stick subtotals on invoices

You need to add a Subtotal item if you ever want to apply a discount to a series of items on an invoice. (I show a Subtotal item on the invoice shown earlier in Figure 2-1.) To add a Subtotal item to your Item list, choose Lists⇨Item List, click the Item button, and select New from the drop-down list. This displays the New Item window — the same window I refer to several times earlier in this chapter. Specify the item type as Subtotal and then provide an item name (such as *Subtotal*).

When you want to subtotal items on an invoice, all you do is stick this Subtotal item on the invoice after the items you want to subtotal. Keep in mind, though, that QuickBooks doesn't set up a subtotal feature automatically. You have to add a Subtotal item; otherwise, you can apply a Discount item that you create only to the single item that immediately precedes the discount. A *Discount item,* by the way, calculates a discount on an invoice.

Creating Group items to batch stuff you sell together

You can create an item that puts one line on an invoice that's actually a combination of several other items. To add a Group item, display the New Item window and specify the item type as Group. QuickBooks displays the New Item window, as shown in Figure 2-5.

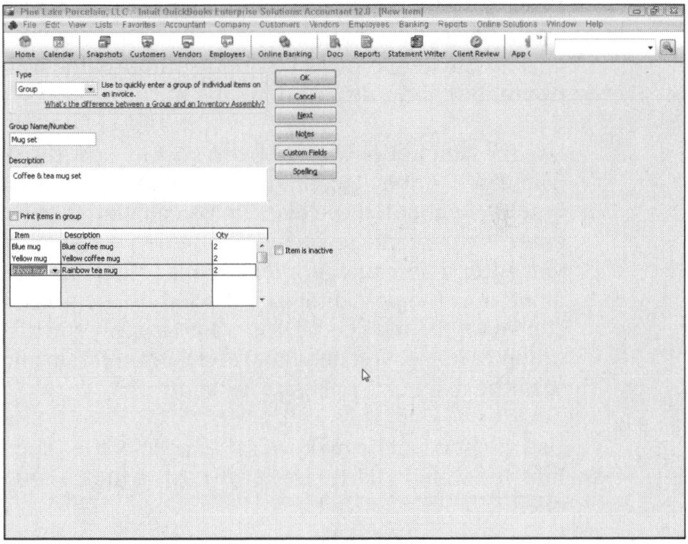

Figure 2-5: The QuickBooks New Item window with the item type Group selected.

For example, if you sell three items — say, blue mugs, yellow mugs, and rainbow mugs — but sometimes sell the items together in a set, you can create an item that groups the three items. Note that when you create a group, you continue to track the group member inventories individually and don't track the inventory of the group as a new item.

In the New Item window, use the Item/Description/Qty list box to list each item included in the group. When you click an item line in the Item/Description/Qty list box, QuickBooks places a down arrow at the right end of the Item column. Click this arrow to open a drop-down list of items. (If the list is longer than can be shown, you can use the scroll bar on the right to move up and down the list.) If you select the Print Items in Group check box, QuickBooks lists all the items in the group on invoices. (In the case of the mugs, invoices list the individual blue, rainbow, and yellow mugs instead of just listing the group name, such as *Mug Set.*)

Creating Discount items to add discounts to invoices

You can create an item that calculates a discount and sticks the discount on an invoice as another line item. (I show a Discount item on the invoice that appears in Figure 2-1.) To add a Discount item to the list, display the New Item window, specify the item type as Discount, and provide an item name or number and a description.

Use the Amount or % text box to specify how the discount is calculated. If the discount is a set amount (such as $50.00), type the amount. If the discount is calculated as a percentage, enter the percentage, including the percent symbol. When you enter a percentage, QuickBooks calculates the discount amount as the percentage multiplied by the preceding item shown on the invoice. (If you want to apply the discount to a group of items, you need to use a Subtotal item and follow it with the discount, as Figure 2-1 shows.)

Use the Account drop-down list to specify the expense account that you want to use to track the cost of the discounts you offer.

Use the Tax Code drop-down list to specify whether the discount gets calculated before or after any sales taxes are calculated. (This option appears only if you indicated in the QuickBooks Setup that you charge sales tax.)

You probably want to check with your local sales tax revenue agency to determine whether sales tax should be calculated before or after the discount.

If you need to collect sales tax, and you didn't set up this function in the QuickBooks Setup, follow these steps:

1. **Choose Edit➪Preferences.**

   The Preferences dialog box appears.

2. **Click the Sales Tax icon in the list on the left, click the Company Preferences tab, and then select the Yes option button in the Do You Charge Sales Tax area.**

3. **Add the Sales Tax item(s) to your Item list.**

Creating Sales Tax Group items to batch sales taxes

Sales Tax Groups enable you to batch several sales taxes that you're supposed to charge as one tax so that they appear as a single sales tax on the invoice. Combining the taxes is necessary — or at least possible — when you're supposed to charge, say, a 6.5 percent state sales tax, a 1.7 percent county sales tax, and a 0.4 percent city sales tax, but you want to show one all-encompassing 8.6 percent sales tax on the invoice.

To add a Sales Tax Group item, display the New Item window and then specify the item type as Sales Tax Group. QuickBooks displays the New Item window, as shown in Figure 2-6. Use the Tax Item/Rate/Tax Agency/Description list box to list the other sales tax items that you want to include in the group. When you click an item line in the list box, QuickBooks places a down arrow at the right end of the Tax Item column. You can click this arrow to open a drop-down list of Sales Tax items.

Editing items

If you make a mistake, you can change any piece of item information by displaying the Item List window and double-clicking the item so that QuickBooks displays the Edit Item window, which you can use to make changes.

Figure 2-6: The New Item window for the item type Sales Tax Group.

The Item List window provides another tool you can use to edit item information. If you click the Item button and choose the Add/Edit Multiple Items command, QuickBooks displays the Add/Edit Multiple List Entries window. This window provides a spreadsheet you can use to add or edit more than one item at a time. The method I describe in the previous paragraphs often works best because it allows you to collect more information — for example, information such as item descriptions. But if you need to enter or edit a large number of items, check out the Add/Edit Multiple Items command. Sometimes the command saves you time.

Adding Employees to Your Employee List

If you do payroll in QuickBooks, or if you track sales by employees, you need to describe each employee. Describing employees is pretty darn easy. Click the Employee Center icon at the top of the screen to display the Employee Center window. Then click the New Employee button that appears just above the list in the upper-left corner of the screen to have QuickBooks display the New Employee window, as shown in Figure 2-7.

When you click the New Employee button, QuickBooks may prompt you to use its Employee Organizer's Hire Employee tool, which walks you through several steps (including a background check), provides sample employment application and payroll tax forms, and collects descriptive information about an employee. You may want to use these tools for new prospective employees (and can do so simply by clicking the buttons and links provided). To skip all the formality or to describe an existing employee, however, click Cancel. To intentionally use the Hire Employee tool, you can also choose the Employees➪Employee Organizer➪Hire Employee command.

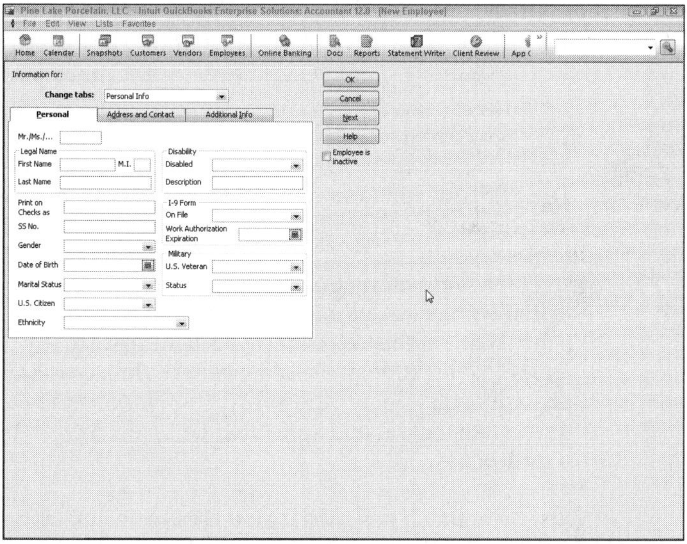

Figure 2-7: The New Employee window.

The New Employee window is pretty straightforward, right? You just fill in the fields to describe the employee.

Lesser computer-book writers would probably provide step-by-step descriptions of how you move the cursor to the First

Name text box and type the person's first name, how you move the cursor to the next text box, type something there, and so on. Not me. No way. I know that you can tell just by looking at this window that all you do is click a text box and type the obvious bit of information. Right?

I do need to tell you a couple of important things about the New Employee window:

> ✓ When you release an employee, it's important to enter the release date for the employee on the Employment Info tab after you write that final paycheck. (To change to a new tab, choose the new tab from the cleverly named Change Tabs drop-down list.) This way, when you process payroll in the future, you can't accidentally pay the former employee.
>
> ✓ As for the Type field (an option on the Employment Info tab), most employees probably fit the regular category. If you're uncertain whether an employee fits the guidelines for corporate officer, statutory employee, or owner, see the *Circular E* publication from the IRS. And sleep tight.

The Address and Contact tab provides boxes for you to collect and store address information. The Additional Info tab enables you to create customizable fields in case you want to keep information that isn't covered by the QuickBooks default fields — favorite color and that type of thing. Again, what you need to do on this tab is fairly straightforward. By the way, if you told QuickBooks that you want to do payroll, QuickBooks prompts you to enter the information it needs to calculate things like federal and state income taxes, payroll taxes, and vacation pay.

After you finish describing an employee, click OK to add the employee to the list and return to the Employee List window, or click Next to add the employee to the list and add more employees.

You can also inactivate an employee from your list if it starts to get cluttered with names of employees who no longer work for you. I recommend waiting to inactivate them until after the year is finished and the W-2 forms have been printed.

Customers Are Your Business

Here's how you add customers to your Customer list:

1. **Choose Customers⇨Customer Center.**

   The Customer Center window appears.

2. **Click the New Customer & Job button and then click New Customer.**

   QuickBooks displays the Address Info tab of the New Customer window, as shown in Figure 2-8. Use this window to describe the customer in as much detail as possible.

   If you click the New Customer button and choose the Add Multiple Customers:Jobs command, QuickBooks displays a worksheet you can use to describe multiple customers at a time.

3. **Type the customer's name.**

   Enter the name of the customer as you want it to appear in the Customer list. You can list customers by company name or by the representative's last name.

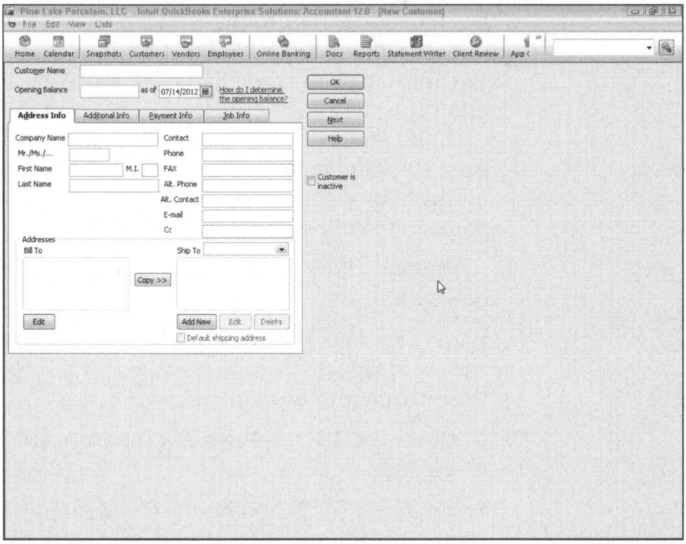

Figure 2-8: The New Customer window.

4. Enter the company name.

5. (Optional) Enter the name of your contact, along with other pertinent information.

Move the cursor to the Mr./Ms. text box and type the appropriate title. Do the same with the First Name, M.I., and Last Name text boxes. (QuickBooks automatically fills in the names in the Contact text box as you type them. Nice touch, eh?)

Go ahead and fill in the Phone, FAX, Alt. Phone, and E-Mail text boxes while you're at it.

6. (Really optional) Type the name of your alternative contact in the Alt. Contact text box.

7. Enter the billing address.

You can use the Bill To text box to provide the customer's billing address. QuickBooks copies the Company and Contact names to the first lines of the billing address, so you need to enter only the address. To move from the end of one line to the start of the next, press Enter.

8. Enter the shipping address.

You can use the Ship To field to provide the customer's shipping address. Click the Copy button to copy the billing address to the Ship To field. If the shipping address differs from the Bill To address, simply open the Ship To drop-down list, click Add New, and then enter the shipping address information the same way that you enter the Bill To address. You can add multiple shipping addresses. After you add a shipping address for a customer, you can select the shipping address from the Ship To drop-down list.

9. (Optional) Click the Additional Info tab and record more data.

When you click this tab, QuickBooks displays the tab shown in Figure 2-9. You can use this tab to describe the customer in more detail.

10. (Optional) Click the Payment Info tab and record more data.

You can use the boxes on the Payment Info tab (see Figure 2-10) to record bits of customer information, such as the account number that should be included with any payments.

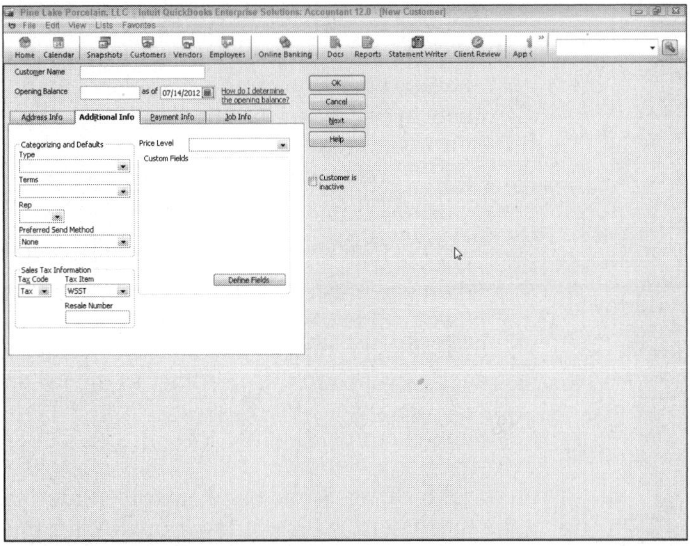

Figure 2-9: Add more details on the Additional Info tab.

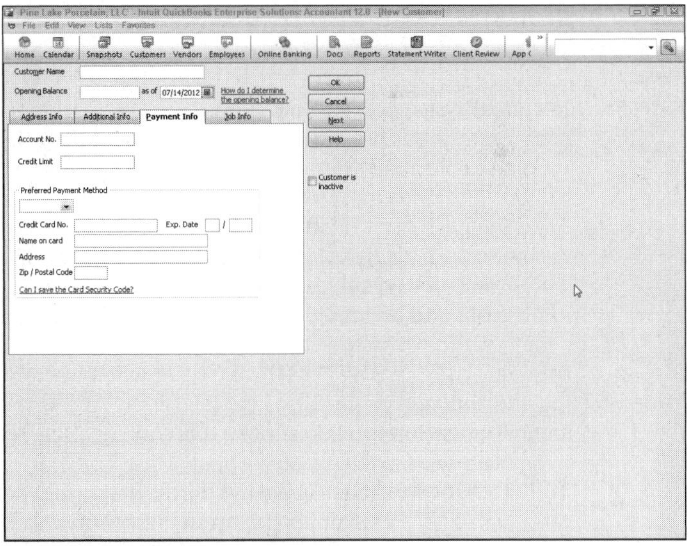

Figure 2-10: The Payment Info tab.

11. **(Optional) Click the Job Info tab to add specific job information.**

    Because you're creating a new customer account, not invoicing by jobs, I explain this step in the next section. If you're the "can't wait" type, feel free to take a look. You can add a specific job to the new customer's information.

12. **Save the customer information by clicking OK or Next.**

    When you finish describing a customer, you can save it in one of two ways: Click OK to add the customer to the list and return to the Customer Center window, or click Next to add the customer to the list and keep the New Customer window onscreen so that you can add more customers.

If you want to change some bit of customer information, display the Customer Center window, double-click the customer name in which you want to change information, and then make changes in the Edit Customer window.

It's Just a Job

In QuickBooks, you can track invoices by customer or by customer and job. This may sound kooky, but some businesses invoice customers (perhaps several times) for specific jobs.

Take the case of a construction subcontractor who does foundation work for a handful of builders of single-family homes. This construction subcontractor probably invoices his customers by job, and he invoices each customer several times for the same job. For example, he invoices Poverty Rock Builders for the foundation job at 1113 Birch Street when he pours the footing and then again when he lays the block. At 1028 Fairview, the same foundation job takes more than one invoice, too.

To set up jobs for customers, you first need to describe the customers (as I explain in the preceding section). Then follow these steps:

1. **Choose Customers⇨Customer Center.**

   QuickBooks displays the Customer Center window.

2. Right-click the customer for whom you want to set up a job, choose Add Job from the contextual menu that appears, and click the Add Job tab.

QuickBooks displays the New Job window (shown in Figure 2-11). You use this window to describe the job. A great deal of the information in this window appears on the invoice.

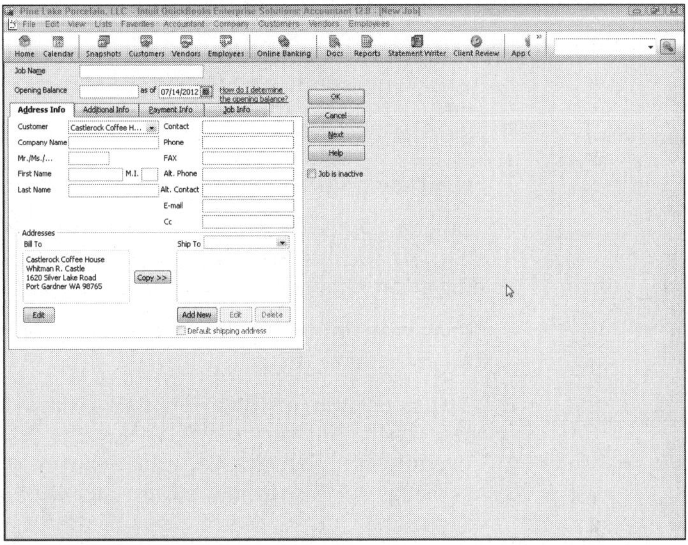

Figure 2-11: The New Job window.

3. Add the job name.

The cursor is in the Job Name text box. Just type the name of the job or project.

4. Identify the customer.

On the off chance that you selected the wrong customer in Step 2, take a peek at the Customer drop-down list. Does it name the correct customer? If not, activate the drop-down list and select the correct customer.

5. (Optional) Name your contact and fill in other relevant information.

You can enter the name of your contact and alternative contact in the Mr./Ms., First Name, M.I., and Last

Name text boxes. QuickBooks fills in the Contact text box for you. You probably don't need to be told this, but fill in the Phone and FAX text boxes just so that you have that information on hand. If you want to get really optional, fill in the Alt. Phone and Alt. Contact text boxes. Go ahead: Take a walk on the wild side.

6. **Enter the job's billing address.**

   You can use the Bill To text box to provide the customer's job billing address. Because chances are good that the job billing address is the same as the customer billing address, QuickBooks copies the billing address from the Customer list. But if need be, make changes.

7. **Select the Ship To address.**

   You can use the Ship To text box to provide the job's shipping address. Click the Copy button if the shipping address is the same as the Bill To address.

8. **(Massively optional) Click the Additional Info tab and categorize the job.**

   You can use the Customer Type drop-down list to give the job type. The only initial types in the default list are Corporate and Referral. You can create other types by choosing Add New from the Customer Type drop-down list (so that QuickBooks displays the New Customer Type dialog box) and then filling in the blanks.

9. **Click the Payment Info tab and set the customer's credit limit (that is, if you've given the customer a credit limit).**

   You can set the customer's credit limit by using the Credit Limit box.

10. **Specify the total of the customer's unpaid invoices by using the Opening Balance text box.**

    Move the cursor to the Opening Balance text box and type the total amount owed by the customer on the conversion date.

QuickBooks suggests that you *not* enter a balance in the Opening Balance box as part of setting up QuickBooks. (If you're interested in the logic of QuickBooks' argument, you can view the Customer's online tutorial, which is available by choosing

Help⇨QuickBooks Learning Center and then clicking the How to Enter Your Customers link.) However, I've thought long and hard about this, and I think you want to enter the customer's unpaid balance into the Opening Balance box. Doing this makes setting up QuickBooks correctly much easier.

11. **Enter the current date in the As Of text box.**

12. **(Optional) Click the Job Info tab and add specific job information.**

    Figure 2-12 shows the Job Info tab. You can use the Job Status drop-down list to choose None, Pending, Awarded, In Progress, Closed, or Not Awarded, whichever is most appropriate. The Start Date is (I know that this one is hard to believe) the day you start the job. As anyone knows, the Projected End and the End Date aren't necessarily the same. Don't fill in the End Date until the job is actually finished. The Job Description field can contain any helpful information you can fit on one line, and the Job Type is an extra field you can use. (If you do use this field, you can add a new job type by choosing Add New from the Job Type list.)

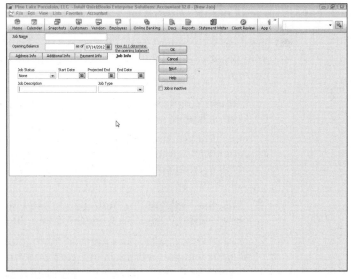

Figure 2-12: The Job Info tab.
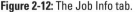

13. Save the job information by clicking OK or Next.

After you finish describing the job, you have two options: You can click OK to add the job to the list and return to the Customer Center window, or you can click Next to add the job to the list and keep the New Job window onscreen so that you can add more jobs.

You can edit job information the same way that you edit customer information. Display the Customer Center window by choosing Customer⇨Customer Center. When QuickBooks displays the window, double-click the job and make the changes in the Edit Job window that appears.

To add a large number of customers or jobs to the Customers list at the same time, display the Customer Center window, click the New Customer & Job button, and then choose the Add Multiple Customer:Jobs option. QuickBooks displays the Add/Edit Multiple List Entries worksheet, which lets you collect and edit all the same information that the regular customer and job windows do.

Adding Vendors to Your Vendor List

Adding vendors to your Vendor list works the same basic way as adding customers to your Customer list. Here's how to get the job done:

1. Choose Vendors⇨Vendor Center or click the Vendor Center icon at the top of the screen.

QuickBooks displays the Vendor Center window. Along with listing your vendors, it lists any sales tax agencies that you identified as part of setting up Sales Tax items.

2. Click the New Vendor button and then choose the New Vendor command from the menu that appears.

QuickBooks displays the Address Info tab of the New Vendor window, as shown in Figure 2-13. You use this window to describe the vendors and all their little idiosyncrasies.

If you click the New Vendor button and choose the Add Multiple Vendors command, QuickBooks displays a worksheet you can use to describe multiple vendors at a time.

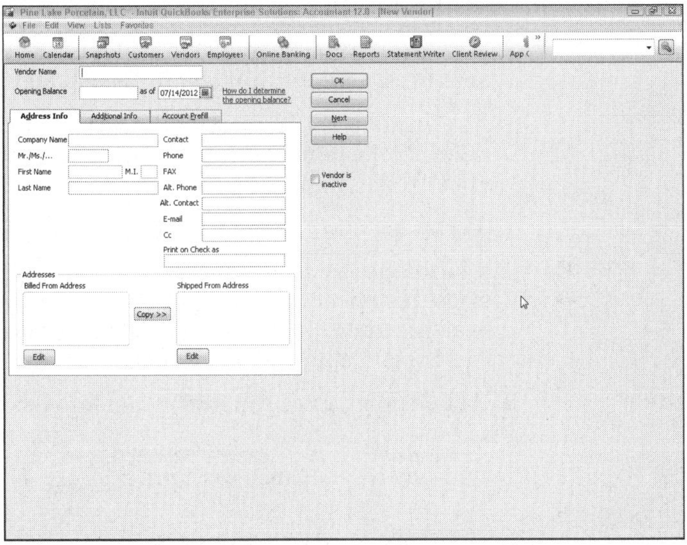

Figure 2-13: The Address Info tab of the New Vendor window.

3. Enter the vendor name.

The cursor is already in the Vendor Name text box. All you have to do is type the vendor's name as you want it to appear on the Vendor list. If you want to list your vendors by company name, enter the company name. To list them by the first or last name of the sales representative, enter one of these names. Just remember that the list is going to sort, alphabetically or numerically, by the information you enter in this field, not by the information below.

4. (Optional) Enter the name of your contact.

Fill in the Mr./Ms., First Name, M.I., and Last Name text boxes. QuickBooks fills in the Contact text box for you automatically.

5. Enter the address to which you're supposed to mail checks.

You can use the Addresses text box to provide the vendor's address. QuickBooks copies the Company and Contact names to the first line of the address, so you need to enter only the street address, city, state, and zip code. To move from the end of one line to the start of the next, press Enter.

6. **(Optional) Enter the vendor's telephone and fax numbers, and, if available, the e-mail address.**

The window also has an Alt. Phone text box for a second telephone number. They thought of everything, didn't they?

7. **Verify the entry in the Print on Check As text box.**

QuickBooks assumes that you want the company name to appear on any checks you write for this vendor. If not, change the text box to whatever you feel is more appropriate.

8. **At this point, click the Additional Info tab.**

The window you see onscreen hopefully bears an uncanny resemblance to Figure 2-14.

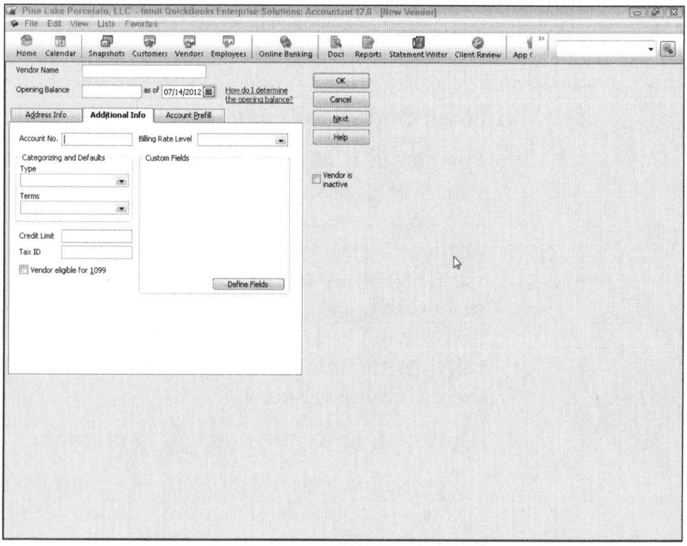

Figure 2-14: The Additional Info tab of the New Vendor window.

9. **(Optional) Enter your account number in the Account No. text box.**

   If the vendor has assigned account numbers or customer numbers to keep track of customers, type your account or customer number in the Account No. text box. You can probably get this piece of information from the vendor's last invoice.

   An account number is required if you want to use QuickBooks' online bill payment feature to pay the vendor. QuickBooks transfers the account number to the memo field of the payment check.

10. **Categorize the vendor by selecting an option from the Type drop-down list.**

    See that Type drop-down list? If you open the list, you see the initial QuickBooks list of vendor types. You can pick any of these types, but my suggestion is that you diligently identify any vendor to whom you need to send a 1099 Form as a 1099 contractor. A *1099 contractor* is any unincorporated business or person who performs services and to whom you pay $600 or more during the year.

    To create a new vendor type, select Add New from the drop-down list and fill in the blanks in the New Vendor Type dialog box that QuickBooks displays. You can create as many new vendor types as you need.

11. **Specify the payment terms that you're supposed to observe by selecting an option from the Terms drop-down list.**

    QuickBooks has already set up all the usual ones. (If you want to, you can choose Add New to set up additional payment terms.)

    If a vendor offers an early payment discount, it's usually too good a deal to pass up. Interested in more information about early payment discounts? Do you have an inquiring mind that needs to know?

12. **(Optional) Specify your credit limit, if the vendor has set one.**

    This procedure is obvious, right? You click in the Credit Limit text box and enter the number.

13. **(If applicable) Store the vendor's federal tax identification number and select the Vendor Eligible for 1099 check box.**

This number might be the vendor's Social Security number if the vendor is a one-person business. If the vendor has employees, the federal tax identification number is the vendor's employer identification number. You need this information only if you're required to prepare a 1099 for the vendor.

14. **Type 0 (zero) in the Opening Balance text box.**

You typically don't want to enter the amount you owe the vendor; you do that later, when you pay your bills. However, if you're using *accrual-basis accounting* for your expenses (this just means that your accounting system counts bills as expenses when you get the bill and not when you pay the bill), you need to tell QuickBooks what amounts you owe vendors at the conversion date. You can do that most easily by entering opening balances for vendors into the Opening Balance box as you set up a vendor in the Vendor list.

15. **Enter the conversion date in the As Of date field.**

What you're doing here, by the way, is providing the date on which the value shown in the Opening Balance text box is correct.

QuickBooks provides an Account Prefill tab on the New Vendor window. Use this tab to specify a set of expense accounts that QuickBooks will suggest any time you indicate you're writing a check, entering a bill, or entering a credit card charge for the vendor.

16. **Save the vendor information by clicking OK or Next.**

After you finish describing the vendor, you have two options: Click OK to add the vendor to the list and return to the Vendor Center window, or click Next to add the vendor to the list and leave the New Vendor window onscreen so that you can add more vendors.

To add a large number of vendors to the Vendor list at the same time, display the Vendor Center window, click the New Vendor button, and then choose the Add Multiple Vendors option. QuickBooks displays the Add/Edit Multiple List

Entries worksheet, which lets you collect and edit all the same information that the regular vendor windows do.

The Other Lists

Throughout the preceding sections, I cover almost all the most important lists. A few others I haven't talked about yet are Fixed Asset, Price Level, Billing Rate Level, Sales Tax Code, Classes, Other Names, Sales Rep, Customer Type, Vendor Type, Job Type, Terms, Customer Messages, Payment Method, Ship Via, and Memorized Transactions. I don't give blow-by-blow descriptions of how you use these lists because you don't really need them. The other QuickBooks lists are generally more than adequate. You can usually use the standard lists as is without building other lists.

Just so I don't leave you stranded, however, I want to give you quick-and-dirty descriptions of these other lists and what they do.

To see some of these lists, choose the list from the Lists menu or choose Lists➪Customer & Vendor Profile Lists and choose the list from the submenu that QuickBooks displays.

The Fixed Asset list

If you buy *fixed assets* — things such as vehicles, various pieces of furniture, miscellaneous hunks of equipment, and so on — somebody is supposed to track this stuff in a list. Why? You need to have this information at your fingertips (or at your accountant's fingertips) to calculate depreciation. And if you later dispose of some item, you need this information to calculate the gain or loss on the sale of the item.

For these reasons, QuickBooks includes a Fixed Asset list. Figure 2-15 shows the Fixed Asset Item List window, used to describe and identify your fixed assets.

Note: I should tell you that your CPA or tax accountant already has such a list that he or she has been maintaining for you. So don't, like, totally freak out because this is the first you've heard about this fixed assets business.

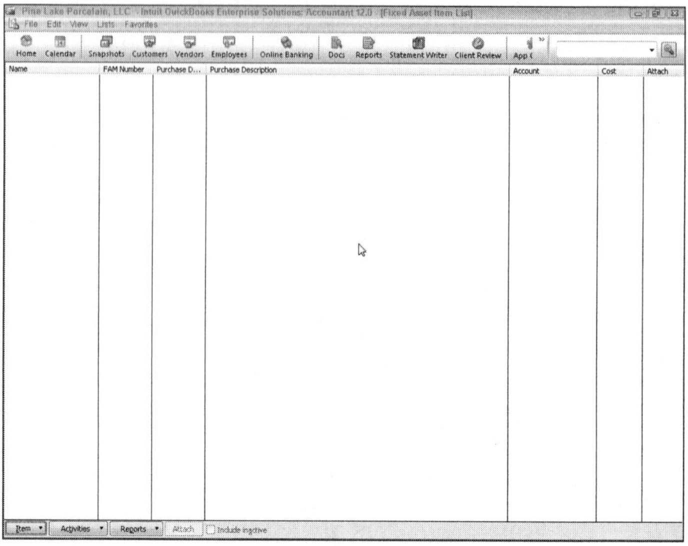

Figure 2-15: The Fixed Asset Item List window.

The Price Level list

The first time I encountered the QuickBooks Price Level fea-ture, I was sorely confused about how the feature worked. I'm still a little confused — not about how the feature works, but about who'd really want to use this feature. But heck, what do I know? Here's the deal: *Price Levels* enable you to adjust an item price as you're creating an invoice. For exam-ple, you can create a price level that increases the price for some item by 20 percent. And you create a price level that decreases the price for some item by 10 percent. You adjust a price by selecting a price level from the Price field on an invoice. (This may not make much sense until you see the Create Invoices window, which I describe in Chapter 3, but it's fairly straightforward.)

The Billing Rate Levels list

The Billing Rate Levels list lets you build a list of custom prices for service items, rather than using just a standard rate for a particular service item. You then use billing rate levels when you invoice a customer for services.

The Sales Tax Code list

The Sales Tax Code list, which appears if you turn on the Sales Tax option, just maintains a list of sales tax codes. These sales tax codes, when used on an invoice or bill, tell QuickBooks whether items are taxable.

The Class list

Classes enable you to classify transactions by department or location, for example, so that you can track trends and assess performance across parts of your business. Classes are cool (really cool), but they add another dimension to the accounting model that you use in QuickBooks, so I'm not going to describe them here. I urge you — nay, I implore you — to get comfortable with how the rest of QuickBooks works before you begin mucking about with classes. Here are just a handful of useful tidbits in case you want to use classes:

- ✔ You may need to turn on the QuickBooks Class Tracking feature. To do this, choose Edit➪Preferences, click the Accounting icon, click the Company Preferences tab, and select the Use Class Tracking check box.

  Note: The Class box appears in data entry windows only after you turn on class tracking.

- ✔ To display the Class list, choose Lists➪Class List.

- ✔ To add classes to the Class list, display the Class List window (choose Lists➪Class List), right-click the window, choose New to display the New Class window, and then fill in the blanks.

- ✔ To tag transactions as falling into a particular class — invoices, checks, bills, journal entries, and so on — select the appropriate class from the Class list box.

By the way, one other point: Before you go off and start using classes to complicate your accounting, make sure that you can't get what you want by beefing up your chart of accounts.

You won't see a Class List command in the Lists menu if you indicated during the QuickBooks Setup that you don't want to use classes. But you can change your mind later and start using classes. Choose Edit➪Preferences, click the Accounting icon, and select the Use Class Tracking check box on the Company Preferences tab.

The Other Names list

QuickBooks provides an Other Names list that works as a watered-down, wimpy Vendor and Employee list combination. You can write checks to people named on this Other Names list, but you can't do anything else. You can't create invoices or purchase orders for them, for example. And you don't get any of the other information that you want to collect for vendors or employees.

You're really better off working with good, accurate, rich Vendor and Employee lists. If you don't like this suggestion, however, just choose Lists⇨Other Names List to display the Other Names List window, click the Other Names button, choose New from the drop-down list, and then fill in the blanks in the New Name window.

The Sales Rep list

You can create a list of the sales representatives you work with and then indicate which sales rep sells to a customer or generates a sale. To do this, choose Lists⇨Customer & Vendor Profile Lists⇨Sales Rep. When you choose this command, QuickBooks displays the Sales Rep List window, which lists all the sales representatives. To add sales representatives, click the Sales Rep button, select New from the drop-down list, and then fill in the window that QuickBooks displays.

Customer, Vendor, and Job Types list

You can create lists of customer types, vendor types, and job types and then use these lists to categorize customer, vendor, and job information. This is probably no surprise, but to do this, you need to use the appropriate command:

✔ Lists⇨Customer & Vendor Profile Lists⇨Customer
   Type List

✔ Lists⇨Customer & Vendor Profile Lists⇨Vendor Type List

✔ Lists⇨Customer & Vendor Profile Lists⇨Job Type List

When you choose one of these commands, QuickBooks
displays the appropriate List window, which lists all the
Customer types, Vendor types, or Job types. To add types,
click the Type button, select New from the drop-down list,
and then fill in the window that QuickBooks displays.

How you use any of these types of lists depends on your
business. In a situation in which you want to sort or segre-
gate customers, vendors, or jobs in some unusual way, use
the Customer Type, Vendor Type, or Job Type list.

The Terms list

QuickBooks maintains a Terms list, which you use to specify
what payment terms are available. To add terms, choose
Lists⇨Customer & Vendor Profile Lists⇨Terms List. When
you choose this command, QuickBooks displays the Terms
List window. To add more terms, click the Terms button,
select New from the drop-down list, and then fill in the
window that QuickBooks displays.

The Customer Message list

This list is another minor player in the QuickBooks drama.
You can stick messages at the bottom of invoices if you first
type the message in the Customer Message list. QuickBooks
provides a handful of boilerplate messages: thank you,
happy holidays, mean people suck, and so on. You can add
more messages by choosing Lists⇨Customer & Vendor
Profile Lists⇨Customer Message List. When QuickBooks
displays the Customer Message List window, click its
Customer Message button and choose New. Then use the
New Customer Message window that QuickBooks displays to
create a new message.

The Payment Method list

Now this will be a big surprise. (I'm just kidding.) QuickBooks provides descriptions for the usual payment methods. But, of course, you can add to these by choosing Lists⇨Customer & Vendor Profile Lists⇨Payment Method. When you choose this command, QuickBooks displays the lost city of Atlantis. Okay, not really. QuickBooks actually displays the Payment Method window. To add more methods, click the Payment Method button, select New from the drop-down list, and then fill in the window that QuickBooks displays.

The Ship Via list

QuickBooks provides descriptions for the usual shipping methods. These descriptions are probably entirely adequate. If you need to add more, however, you can do so by choosing Lists⇨Customer & Vendor Profile Lists⇨Ship Via. When you choose this command, QuickBooks displays the Ship Via List window, which lists all the shipping methods that you or QuickBooks said are available. To add more methods, click the Shipping Method button, select New from the drop-down list, and then fill in the window that QuickBooks displays. Friends, it doesn't get much easier than this.

The Vehicle list

QuickBooks provides a Vehicle list that you can use to maintain a list of business vehicles. To see the Vehicle list, choose Lists⇨Customer & Vendor Profile Lists⇨Vehicle List. When you choose this command, QuickBooks displays the Vehicle List window, which lists all the vehicles that you previously said are available. To identify additional vehicles, click the Vehicle button, select New from the drop-down list, and then fill in the window that QuickBooks displays.

To record vehicle mileage inside QuickBooks, choose Company⇨Enter Vehicle Mileage. Then use the window that QuickBooks displays to identify the vehicle, the trip length in miles, the trip date, and a bit of other trip-related information.

The Memorized Transaction list

The Memorized Transaction list isn't really a list. At least, it's not like the other lists that I describe in this chapter. The Memorized Transaction list is a list of accounting transactions — invoices, bills, checks, purchase orders, and so on — that you've asked QuickBooks to memorize. To display the Memorized Transaction list, choose Lists⇨Memorized Transaction List.

You can have QuickBooks memorize transactions so that you can quickly record them later or even put them on a schedule for recurring usage. This feature can save you lots of time, especially for transactions you regularly make.

The Reminders list

Here's a list that isn't accessible from the Lists menu. QuickBooks keeps track of a bunch of stuff that it knows you need to monitor. If you choose Company⇨Reminders, QuickBooks displays the Reminders window. Here, you see such entries as invoices and checks that need to be printed, inventory items you should probably reorder, and so on.

Organizing Lists

To organize a list, you must be in single-user mode. Here are some ways that you can organize your list:

- ✔ **To move an item and all its subitems:** Click the diamond beside the item and then drag the item up or down the list to a new location.

- ✔ **To make a subitem its own item:** Click the diamond beside the item and then drag it to the left.

- ✔ **To make an item a subitem:** Move the item so that it's directly beneath the item you want it to fall under. Then click the diamond beside the item and drag it to the right.

- ✔ **To alphabetize a list:** Click the Name button at the top of the list window. QuickBooks alphabetizes your list of customers, vendors, accounts and so on in both "a to z" order and reverse "z to a" order.

You can't reorganize the Vendor or the Employee list.

Printing Lists

You can print customer, vendor, and employee lists by clicking the Print button at the top of the specific Center screen for the type of list you choose. The list is among the options available to print in a drop-down list.

You can print a regular list by displaying the list, clicking the button in the lower-left corner of the list window, and then choosing Print List. However, often the best way to print a list is to print a list report. You can create, customize, and print a list report by choosing Reports⇨List and then choosing the list that you want to print. You can also create one of a handful of list reports by clicking the Reports button in the list window and choosing a report from the pop-up menu.

Click the Activities button in a list window to quickly access common activities associated with the items on that list. Or click Reports to quickly access common reports related to the items on the list.

Exporting List Items to Your Word Processor

If you use QuickBooks to store the names and addresses of your customers, vendors, and employees, you can create a text file of the contact information for these people. You can then export this file to another application, such as a word processor, to create reports that use this information.

To export list information to a text file, click the button in the lower-left corner of the list window and choose Print List. When QuickBooks displays the Print dialog box, select the File option button, click Print, and then provide a filename when prompted.

The File menu Print Forms command also provides a Labels command for producing mailing labels for customers and vendors. And before I forget, let me also mention that the last command of the Company menu — Prepare Letters with

Envelopes — lets you prepare letters (and, duh, addressed envelopes) from the name and address information from the Customer, Vendor, and Employee lists discussed earlier in this chapter.

Dealing with the Chart of Accounts List

I saved the best for last. After you get done setting up your lists, you still need to finalize one list: the Chart of Accounts. The Chart of Accounts just lists the accounts you and QuickBooks use to track income and expenses, assets, liabilities, and equity.

This is kind of a funny step, however, because a bunch of Chart of Accounts stuff is already set up. So what you're really doing here is just finalizing the chart of accounts. Typically, this consists of two or possibly three separate steps: describing customer balances, describing vendor balances, and entering the rest of the trial balance.

Describing customer balances

If you entered customer unpaid invoice totals when you set up the customers — which is what I recommend — you've already described your customer balances. You, my friend, can skip ahead to the next section, "Describing vendor balances."

If you didn't enter customer unpaid invoice totals, you need to supply that information before you finalize the Chart of Account information. To do this, enter the invoice in the usual way, which I describe in Chapter 3. The one really important thing to do is use the original invoice date when you enter the invoice.

Now, I know what you're thinking: "Hey, dude. The order of your instructions is all screwed up. Here I am, slogging through Chapter 2, and now totally out of the blue, you're telling me that I have to jump ahead to Chapter 3 and read that?"

Yeah, well, that's right. This jumping around and jumping ahead is the big reason that I told you earlier to do it the way I did. Hey, sorry.

Describing vendor balances

If you entered vendor unpaid bill totals when you set up the vendors — this is also what I recommend — you described your vendor balances.

If you didn't enter vendor unpaid bill totals, you need to supply that information, as I describe in Chapter 5 in the discussion on recording your bills the accounts payable way. The one really important thing to do is to use the original vendor bill date when you enter the vendor bill.

Camouflaging some accounting goofiness

After you enter the customer and vendor balances into QuickBooks, you need to enter the rest of the trial balance, which you do by taking two big steps. In the first step, you camouflage a couple of goofy accounts, called *suspense accounts,* which QuickBooks creates when you set up the Item, Customer, and Vendor lists. The second step, which I describe in the following section, is supplying the last few missing numbers.

Figure 2-16 shows a sample trial balance after I enter the inventory, accounts receivable, and accounts payable balances. When you set up your Item, Customer, and Vendor lists, you also create account balances for inventory, accounts receivable, and accounts payable.

You can produce your own half-complete trial balance from inside QuickBooks by clicking the Report Center icon and choosing Reports⇨Accountants & Taxes⇨Trial Balance. QuickBooks displays the trial balance report in a document window.

If you need to do so, enter the conversion date in the As Of box by clicking in the box and typing the conversion date in MM/DD/YYYY format. Figure 2-16, for example, shows the conversion date 6/30/2012 on the As Of line. You can set the From box to any value; the From and To range just needs to end with the conversion date. Make a note of the credit and debit balances shown for the Uncategorized Income and Uncategorized Expenses accounts.

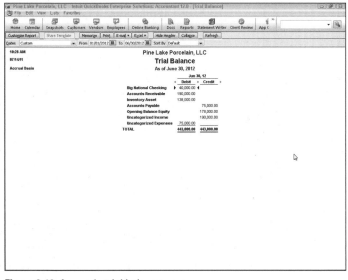

Figure 2-16: A sample trial balance.

If you want, you can print the report by clicking the Print button; then, when QuickBooks displays the Print Report dialog box, click its Print button. Yes, you click *two* Print buttons.

After you have the conversion date balances for the Uncategorized Income and Uncategorized Expenses accounts, you're ready to make the accrual-accounting adjustment. To do so, follow these steps:

1. **From the Home screen, either click the Chart of Accounts icon in the Company area or choose Lists⇨Chart of Accounts to display the Chart of Accounts window, as shown in Figure 2-17.**

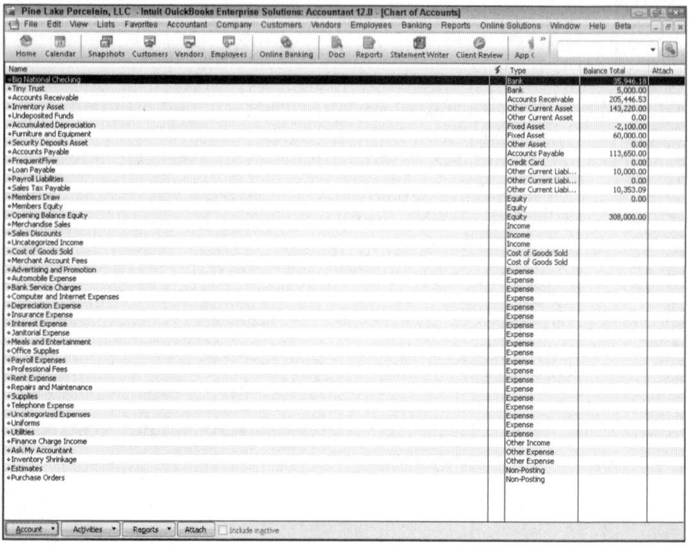

Figure 2-17: The Chart of Accounts window.

2. **Double-click Opening Balance Equity in the Chart of Accounts list to display that account.**

   Opening Balance Equity is listed after the liability accounts. QuickBooks displays the *register* — just a list of transactions — for the Opening Balance Equity account. Figure 2-18, coincidentally, shows this register.

3. **Select the next empty row of the register if it isn't already selected (although it probably is).**

   You can select a row by clicking it, or you can use the up- or down-arrow key to move to the next empty row.

4. **Type the conversion date in the Date field.**

   Move the cursor to the Date field (if it isn't already there), and type the date. Use the MM/DD/YYYY format. For example, you can type either **06302012** or **6/30/2012** to enter June 30, 2012.

5. **Type the Uncategorized Income account balance (from the trial balance report) in the Increase field.**

   In Figure 2-16, for example, the Uncategorized Income account balance is $190,000. In this case, click the Increase field and type **190000** in the field.

You don't need to include the dollar sign or the comma; QuickBooks adds the punctuation for you.

6. **Type** Uncategorized Income **(the account name) in the Account field.**

   Select the Account field, which is on the row under the word *Payee,* and begin typing **Uncategorized Income**, the account name. As soon as you type enough of the name for QuickBooks to figure out what you're typing, it fills in the rest of the name for you. When this happens, you can stop typing.

7. **Click the Record button to record the Uncategorized Income adjustment transaction.**

8. **Again, select the next empty row of the register.**

   Click the row or use the up- or down-arrow key.

9. **Type the conversion date in the Date field.**

   Move the cursor to the Date field (if it isn't already there), and type the date. You use the MM/DD/YYYY format. You can type **6/30/2012**, for example, to enter June 30, 2012.

10. **Type the Uncategorized Expenses account balance in the Decrease field.**

    In Figure 2-16 (shown earlier), for example, the Uncategorized Expenses account balance is $75,000. In this case, you click the Decrease field and then type **75000**. I've said this before, but I'll say it again because you're just starting out: You don't need to include any punctuation, such as a dollar sign or comma.

11. **Type** Uncategorized Expenses **(the account name) in the Account field.**

    Select the Account field, which is on the second line of the register transaction, and begin typing **Uncategorized Expenses**, the account name. As soon as you type enough of the name for QuickBooks to figure out what you're typing, it fills in the rest of the name for you.

12. **Click the Record button to record the Uncategorized Expenses adjustment transaction.**

Figure 2-18 shows the Opening Balance Equity register with the correction transactions. The correction transactions are numbered with a 1 and a 2. See them? They're the third and fourth transactions in the register.

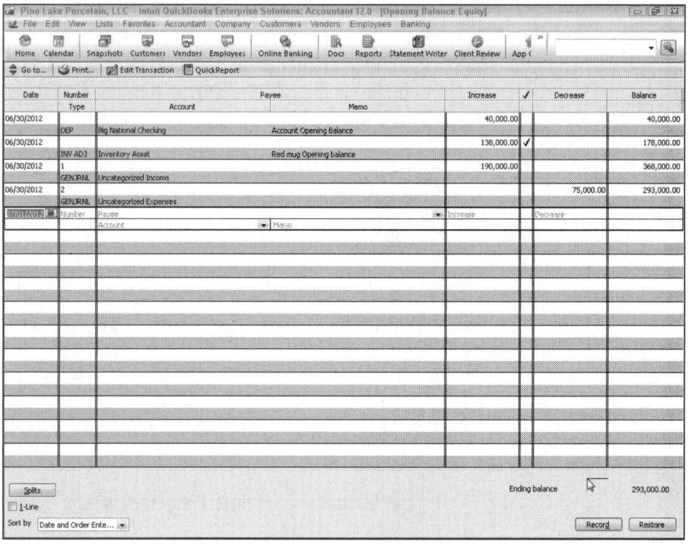

Figure 2-18: The transactions numbered 1 and 2 fix the uncategorized income and uncategorized expenses account balances.

You can close the Opening Balance Equity register at this point. You're finished with it. One way to close it is to click the Close button in the upper-right corner of the window.

You can check your work thus far — and checking it *is* a good idea — by producing another copy of the trial balance report. What you want to check are the Uncategorized Income and Uncategorized Expenses account balances. They should both be zero, as shown in Figure 2-19.

You can produce a trial balance by choosing Reports⇨ Accountant & Taxes⇨Trial Balance. QuickBooks displays the trial balance report in a document window. If you need to enter the conversion date in the As Of line, click the box and type the conversion date in MM/DD/YYYY format.

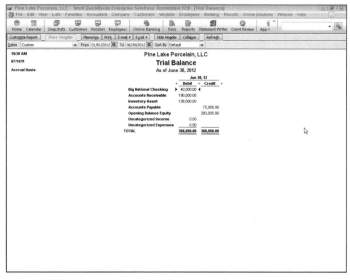

Figure 2-19: Another sample trial balance.

If the Uncategorized Income and the Uncategorized Expenses account balances don't show zero, you (with my help, of course) might have botched the accrual adjustment. To fix the mistake, redisplay the Opening Balance Equity register (as noted earlier, you can double-click Opening Balance Equity in the Chart of Accounts list to display that account), select the adjustment transactions, and then check the account, amount, and field (Increase or Decrease). If one of the fields is wrong, select the field and replace its contents by typing over it.

Supplying the missing numbers

You're almost done. Really. Your last task is to enter the rest of the trial balance amounts into QuickBooks. To perform this task, you need to have a trial balance prepared as of the conversion date. If you followed my instructions in Chapter 1, you have one. Follow these steps:

1. **Choose either Company⇨Make Journal Entries or Accountant⇨Make Journal Entries.**

   QuickBooks displays the Make General Journal Entries window, as shown in Figure 2-20.

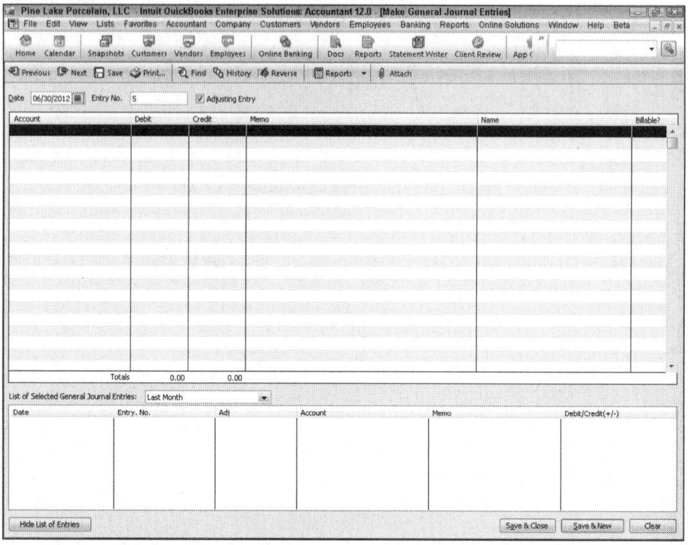

Figure 2-20: The empty Make General Journal Entries window.

2. **Type the conversion date in the Date field.**

   Move the cursor to the Date field (if it isn't already there) and type the date. As you might know by now, you use the MM/DD/YYYY format. For example, type **6/30/2012** for June 30, 2012 (or **06302012** if you don't want to put in the slashes).

3. **Type each trial balance account and balance that isn't already in the half-completed trial balance.**

   Okay. This step sounds confusing. But remember that you've already entered your cash, accounts receivable, inventory, and accounts payable account balances, and perhaps even a few other account balances and a portion of the Opening Bal Equity account balance as part of the QuickBooks Setup.

   Now you need to enter the rest of the trial balance — specifically, the year-to-date income and expense account balances, any missing assets or liabilities, and the remaining portion of the Opening Bal Equity. To enter each account and balance, use a row of the Make General Journal Entries window list box. Figure 2-21 shows how this window looks after you enter the rest of the trial balance into the list box rows.

If you need an account that isn't already on your QuickBooks chart of accounts, no problem. Enter the account name you want into the Account column of the Make General Journal Entries window. When QuickBooks displays the message `Account not found`, click the Set Up button. QuickBooks then displays the Add New Account: Choose Account Type dialog box. Use it to identify the type of account you're setting up: Income, Expense, Fixed Asset, Bank, Loan, Credit, or Equity. Click Continue to display the Add New Account dialog box. Use it to create a longer description of the account (if you want) and then click Save & Close.

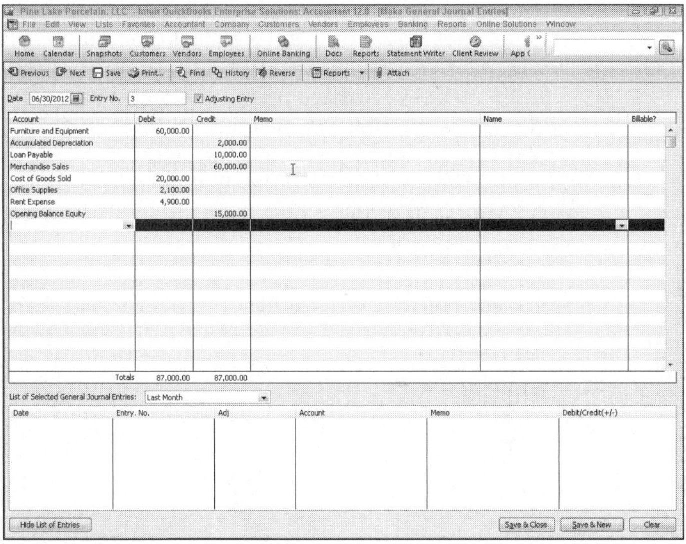

Figure 2-21: The completed Make General Journal Entries window.

4. **Click the Save & New button to record the general journal entries that set up the rest of your trial balance.**

Checking your work one more time

Double-checking your work is a good idea. Produce another copy of the trial balance report. Check that the QuickBooks trial balance is the same one that you wanted to enter.

You can produce a trial balance by choosing Reports⇨ Accountant & Taxes⇨Trial Balance. Be sure to enter the conversion date in the As Of text box. If the QuickBooks trial balance report agrees with what your records show, you're finished.

If the QuickBooks trial balance doesn't agree with what your records show, you need to fix the problem. Fixing it is a bit awkward but isn't complicated. Choose Reports⇨Accountant & Taxes⇨Journal. QuickBooks displays a report or journal that lists all the transactions that you or QuickBooks entered as part of setting up. (The Dates, From, and To text boxes need to specify the conversion date.) Scroll through the list of transactions until you get to the last one. The last transaction is the one that you entered to set up the rest of the trial balance; it names recognizable accounts and uses familiar debit and credit amounts. Double-click this transaction. QuickBooks redisplays the Make General Journal Entries window with the botched transaction. Find the mistake and then fix the erroneous account or amount by clicking it and typing the correct account or amount.

Congratulations! You're done.

Chapter 3

Creating Invoices and Credit Memos

In This Chapter

▶ Deciding whether you're ready to invoice your customers

▶ Preparing invoices and credit memos

▶ Fixing invoice and credit memo mistakes

▶ Printing invoices and credit memos one at a time

▶ Printing invoices and credit memos in a batch

▶ Sending your invoices and credit memos via e-mail

▶ Customizing invoices and credit memos

*I*n this chapter (you might be surprised to discover), I describe how to create and print invoices in QuickBooks as well as how to create and print credit memos.

You use the QuickBooks invoice form to bill customers for the goods that you sell. You use its credit memos form to handle returns and canceled orders for which you've received payments.

Making Sure That You're Ready to Invoice Customers

I know that you're probably all set to go. But first, you need to check a few things, okay? Good.

You already should have installed QuickBooks, of course. You should have set up a company and a Chart of Accounts in the QuickBooks Setup, as I describe in Chapter 1. You also should have entered all your lists and your starting trial balance or talked your accountant into entering it for you, as I describe in Chapter 2.

As long as you've done all this prerequisite stuff, you're ready to start. If you don't have one of the prerequisites done, you need to complete it before going any further.

Sorry. I don't make the rules. I just tell you what they are.

Preparing an Invoice

After you complete all the preliminary work, preparing an invoice with QuickBooks is a snap. If clicking buttons and filling in text boxes are becoming old hat to you, skip the following play-by-play commentary and simply display the Create Invoices window — by either choosing Customers⟶Create Invoices or clicking the Invoices icon on the Home page — and then fill in this window and click the Print button. If you want more help than a single sentence provides, keep reading for step-by-step instructions.

In the following steps, I describe how to create the most complicated and involved invoice around: a *product invoice.* Some fields on the product invoice don't appear on the *service* or *professional invoice,* but don't worry whether your business is a service or professional. Creating a service or professional invoice works basically the same way as creating a product invoice — you just fill in fewer fields. And keep in mind that you start with Steps 1 and 2 no matter what type of invoice you create. Without further ado, here's how to create an invoice:

1. **Display the Create Invoices window by choosing Customers⟶Create Invoices.**

   The Create Invoices window appears, as shown in Figure 3-1.

2. **Select the template or invoice form that you want to use from the Template drop-down list located in the upper-right corner.**

QuickBooks comes with predefined invoice form types, including Product, Professional, Service, and (depending on how you set up QuickBooks and which version of QuickBooks you're using) a handful of other specialized invoice templates as well. Which one appears by default depends on which one you told QuickBooks that you wanted to use in the QuickBooks Setup. You can even create your own custom invoice template (or modify an existing one) by clicking the Customize button. I describe customizing invoice forms in the "Customizing Your Invoices and Credit Memos" section, later in this chapter.

3. **Identify the customer and, if necessary, the job by using the Customer:Job drop-down list.**

   Scroll through the Customer:Job drop-down list until you see the customer or job name that you need; then click it.

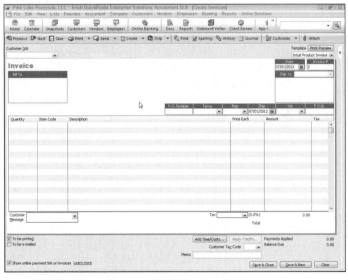

Figure 3-1: The Create Invoices window.

4. **(Optional) Assign a class to the invoice.**

   If you use classes to track expenses and income, activate the Class drop-down list and select an appropriate class for the invoice. To turn this handy way of categorizing transactions on or off (which is overkill for some businesses), choose Edit⇨Preferences, click Accounting on the left, click the Company Preferences tab, and then select or clear the Use Class Tracking check box. (Figure 3-1 doesn't show the Class box.)

5. **Give the invoice date.**

   Press Tab several times to move the cursor to the Date text box. Then enter the correct date in MM/DD/YYYY format. You also can use the following secret codes to change the date:

   - *Press* + (the plus symbol) to move the date ahead one day.

   - *Press* – (the minus symbol) to move the date back one day.

   - *Press T* to change the date to today's date (as specified by the system time that your computer's internal clock provides).

   - *Press M* to change the date to the first day of the month (because *M* is the first letter in the word *month*).

   - *Press H* to change the date to the last day of the month (because *H* is the last letter in the word *month*).

   - *Press Y* to change the date to the first day of the year (because, as you no doubt can guess, *Y* is the first letter in the word *year*).

   - *Press R* to change the date to the last day of the year (because *R* is the last letter in the word *year*).

   You can also click the button on the right side of the Date field to display a small calendar. To select a date from the calendar, just click the date you want. Click the arrows in the top-left and top-right corners of the calendar to display the previous or next month.

6. **(Optional) Enter an invoice number in the Invoice # text box.**

   QuickBooks suggests an invoice number by adding 1 to the last invoice number that you used. You can accept this addition, or if you need to have it your way, you can tab to the Invoice # text box and change the number to whatever you want.

7. Fix the Bill To address, if necessary.

QuickBooks grabs the billing address from the Customer list. You can change the address for the invoice by replacing some portion of the usual billing address. You can, for example, insert another line that says *Attention: William Bobbins,* if that's the name of the person to whom the invoice should go.

8. Fix the Ship To address, if necessary.

I feel like a broken record, but here's the deal: QuickBooks also grabs the shipping address from the Customer list. So if the shipping address has something unusual about it for just this one invoice, you can change the address by replacing or adding information to the Ship To address block. Note that QuickBooks will keep track of each of the shipping addresses you use for a customer, so if you used a shipping address before, you may be able to select it from the Ship To drop-down list.

9. (Optional . . . sort of) Provide the purchase order number in the P.O. Number text box.

If the customer issues purchase orders (POs), enter the number of the purchase order that authorizes this purchase. (Just for the record, PO is pronounced *pee-oh,* not *poh* or *poo.*)

10. Specify the payment terms by selecting an option from the Terms drop-down list.

11. (Optional) Name the sales representative.

Rep doesn't stand for *Reputation,* so don't put three-letter editorial comments in here (although I can't, for the life of me, imagine what you could do with three letters). If you want to track sales by sales representative, use the Rep drop-down list. Simply activate the list by clicking its arrow and then pick a name. Sales representatives can include employees, but they can also include other people whom you've entered in your other lists. To quickly add a sales rep, select Add New and then use the handy-dandy dialog boxes that

QuickBooks displays. To work with the Sales Rep list, choose Lists➪Customer & Vendor Profile Lists➪Sales Rep List.

12. Specify the shipping date if it's something other than the invoice date.

To specify the date, simply move the cursor to the Ship text box and then type the date in MM/DD/YYYY format. You can move the cursor by pressing Tab or by clicking the text box.

Oh — one other quick point: Remember all those secret codes that I talk about in Step 5 for changing the invoice date? They also work for changing the shipping date.

13. Specify the shipping method.

You can probably guess how you specify the shipping method, but parallel structure and a compulsive personality force me to continue. So to specify the shipping method, move the cursor to the Via drop-down list and then select a shipping method from it.

By the way, you can add new shipping methods to the list by selecting Add New and then filling out the cute little dialog box that QuickBooks displays. Setting up new shipping methods is really easy. Really easy.

14. Specify the FOB point by using the F.O.B. text box.

FOB stands for *free-on-board*. The FOB point is more important than it first seems — at least in a business sense — because the FOB point determines when the transfer of ownership occurs, who pays freight, and who bears the risks of damage to the goods during shipping.

If a shipment is free-on-board at the *shipping* point, the ownership of the goods being sold transfers to the purchaser as soon as the goods leave the seller's shipping dock. (Remember that you're the seller.) In this case, the purchaser pays the freight and bears the risk of shipping damage. You can specify the FOB shipping point either as FOB Shipping Point or by using the name of the city. If the shipping point is Seattle, for example, FOB Seattle is the same thing as FOB Shipping Point. Most goods are shipped as FOB Shipping Point, by the way.

If a shipment is free-on-board at the *destination* point, the ownership of the goods that are being sold transfers to the purchaser as soon as the goods arrive on the purchaser's shipping dock. The seller pays the freight and bears the risk of shipping damage. You can specify the FOB destination point either as FOB Destination Point or by using the name of the city. If the destination point is Omaha, for example, FOB Omaha is the same thing as FOB Destination Point.

15. Enter each item that you're selling.

Move the cursor to the first row of the Quantity/Item Code/Description/Price Each/Amount/Tax list box. Okay, I know that isn't a very good name for it, but you know what I mean, right? You need to start filling in the line items that go on the invoice. After you move the cursor to a row in the list box, QuickBooks turns the Item Code field into a drop-down list. Activate the Item Code drop-down list of the first empty row in the list box and then select the item.

When you select the item, QuickBooks fills in the Description and Price Each text boxes with whatever sales description and sales price you've entered in the Item list. (You can edit the information for this particular invoice if you need to.) Enter the number of items sold in the Quantity text box. (After you enter this number, QuickBooks calculates the amount by multiplying Quantity by Price Each.) If you need other items on the invoice, use the remaining empty rows of the list box to enter each one. If you marked the Taxable check box when you added the item to the Item list, the word *Tax* appears in the Tax column to indicate that the item will be taxed. If the item is nontaxable (or you feel like being a tax evader for no good reason), click the Tax column and select *Non.*

Click the Add Time/Costs button at the bottom of the form to display the Choose Billable Time and Costs dialog box. Use this dialog box to select costs that you've assigned to the customer or job. Use the Items tab to select items purchased for the job. Use the Expenses tab to select reimbursable expenses and enter markup information. Use the Time tab to select billable time recorded by the Timer program, the Weekly Timesheet, or in the Time/Enter Single Activity window.

16. **Enter any special items that the invoice should include.**

    If you haven't worked much with the QuickBooks item file, you have no idea what I'm talking about. (For more information about adding to and working with lists in QuickBooks, cruise through Chapter 2.)

    To describe any of the special items, activate the Item Code drop-down list of the next empty row and then select the special item. After QuickBooks fills in the Description and Price Each text boxes, edit this information (if necessary). Describe each of the other special items — subtotals, discounts, freight, and so on — that you're itemizing on the invoice by filling in the empty rows in the list box.

    If you want to include a Discount item and have it apply to multiple items, you need to stick a Subtotal item on the invoice after the inventory or other items that you want to discount. Then stick a Discount item directly after the Subtotal item. QuickBooks calculates the discount as a percentage of the subtotal.

17. **(Optional) Add a customer message.**

    Click in the Customer Message box, activate its drop-down list, and select a clever customer message. To add customer messages to the Customer Message list, choose Add New and then fill in the dialog box that QuickBooks displays. (I know that I talk about the Customer Message box in Chapter 2, but I wanted to quickly describe how to add a customer message again so that you don't have to flip back through a bunch of pages.)

18. **Specify the sales tax.**

    If you specified a tax rate in the Customer list, QuickBooks uses it as a default. If it isn't correct, move the cursor to the Tax list box, activate the drop-down list, and select the correct sales tax.

19. **(Truly optional) Add a memo.**

    You can add a memo description to the invoice if you want to. This memo doesn't print on invoices — only on the Customer Statement. Memo descriptions give you a way of storing information related to an invoice with that invoice. Figure 3-2 shows a completed Create Invoices window.

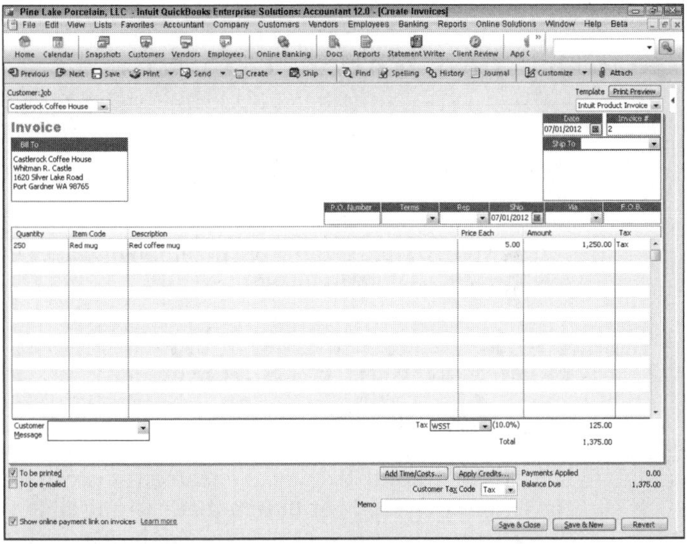

Figure 3-2: A completed Create Invoices window.

20. **If you want to delay printing this invoice, clear the To Be Printed check box that's below the column of buttons in the lower-left area of the Create Invoices window.**

    I want to postpone talking about what selecting the To Be Printed check box does until I finish the discussion of invoice creation. I talk about printing invoices a little later in the chapter. I promise.

21. **Save the invoice by clicking the Save & New button or the Save & Close button.**

    QuickBooks saves the invoice that's onscreen. If you click Save & New, QuickBooks displays an empty Create Invoices window so that you can create another invoice.

    You can page back and forth through invoices that you created earlier by clicking the Next and Previous buttons.

When you're done creating invoices, you can click the invoice form's Save & Close button. Or click the Close button, also known as the Close box, which is the little red box marked with an X in the upper-right corner of the window.

Fixing Invoice Mistakes

I'm not a perfect person. You're not a perfect person. Heck, nobody is; everyone makes mistakes. You don't need to get worked up over mistakes that you make while entering information in invoices, though, because in the following sections, I show you how to fix the most common mistakes that you might make on your invoices.

If the invoice is still displayed onscreen

If the invoice is still displayed onscreen, you can just move the cursor to the box or button that's wrong and then fix the mistake. Because most of the bits of information that you enter in the Create Invoices window are short and sweet, you can easily replace the contents of some fields by typing over whatever's already there. To start all over again, just click the Clear button. To save the invoice after you've made your changes, click the Save & New button.

If you need to insert a line in the middle of the invoice, right-click to display a contextual menu and then choose Insert Line or Delete Line.

If the invoice isn't displayed onscreen

If the invoice isn't displayed onscreen and you haven't yet printed it, you can use the Next and Previous buttons to page through the invoices. When you get to the one with the error, simply fix the error as I describe in the preceding section. If you make an error fixing the invoice, you can click the Revert button to go back to the saved invoice. The Revert button replaces the Clear button when you're viewing an existing invoice — that is, an invoice that you've already saved.

If you printed the invoice, you also can make the sort of change that I describe in the preceding paragraphs. For example, you can page through the invoices until you find the one (now printed) that has the error. And you can correct the error and print the invoice again. I'm not so sure that you want to go this route, however, if you've already sent the invoice. You might want to consider fixing the invoice by issuing either a credit memo (if the original invoice overcharged) or another invoice (if the original invoice undercharged). The reason why I suggest issuing a credit memo (which I show you how to do in the appropriately titled section, "Preparing a Credit Memo," later in this chapter) or another invoice is that life gets awfully messy if you and your customer have multiple copies of the same invoice floating around and causing confusion.

Deleting an invoice

I hesitate to mention this, but you also can delete invoices. Procedurally, deleting an invoice is easy. You just display the invoice in the Create Invoices window and choose Edit⇨Delete Invoice. When QuickBooks asks you to confirm your deletion, click Yes. Read the following paragraph first, though, because you may not want to delete the invoice.

Even though deleting invoices is easy, it isn't something that you should do casually or for fun. Deleting an invoice is okay if you've just created it, only you have seen it, and you haven't yet printed it. In this case, no one needs to know that you've made a mistake. It's your secret. The rest of the time — even if you create an invoice that you don't want later — you should keep a copy of the invoice in the QuickBooks system. By doing so, you have a record that the invoice existed, which usually makes it easier to answer questions later.

"But how do I correct my books if I leave the bogus invoice?" you ask.

Good question. To correct your financial records for the invoice that you don't want to count anymore, simply *void* the invoice. The invoice remains in the QuickBooks system, but QuickBooks doesn't count it because it loses its quantity and amount information. Good news — voiding an invoice is as simple as deleting one. Just display the invoice in the Create Invoices window and then choose Edit➪Void Invoice.

Preparing a Credit Memo

Credit memos can be a handy way to fix data-entry mistakes that you didn't find or correct earlier. Credit memos are also handy ways to handle things like customer returns and refunds. If you've prepared an invoice or two in your time, you'll find that preparing a QuickBooks credit memo is a lot easier than using old-fashioned methods.

In the following steps, I describe how to create the most complicated and involved kind of credit memo: a *product credit memo*. Creating a *service* or *professional credit memo* works basically the same way, however. You just fill in fewer fields.

1. **Choose Customers➪Create Credit Memos/Refunds or click the Refunds & Credits icon in the Customer section of the Home page to display the Create Credit Memos/Refunds window (as shown in Figure 3-3).**

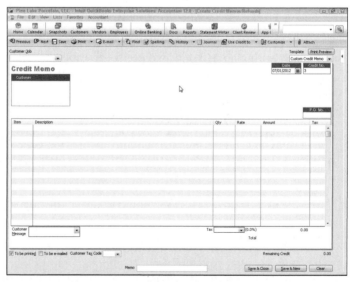

Figure 3-3: The Create Credit Memos/Refunds window.

2. **Identify the customer and, if necessary, the job in the Customer:Job drop-down list.**

   You can select the customer or job from the list by clicking it.

3. **(Optional) Specify a class for the credit memo.**

   If you're using classes to categorize transactions, activate the Class drop-down list and choose the appropriate class for the credit memo.

4. **Date the credit memo. (Going steady is optional.)**

   Press Tab to move the cursor to the Date text box. Then enter the correct date in MM/DD/YYYY format. You also can use the secret date-editing codes that I describe in the section "Preparing an Invoice," earlier in the chapter. Oh, boy.

5. **(Optional) Enter a credit memo number.**

   QuickBooks suggests a credit memo number by adding 1 to the last credit memo number you used. You can accept the number or tab to the Credit No. text box to change the number to whatever you want.

6. **Fix the Customer address, if necessary.**

   QuickBooks grabs the billing address from the Customer list. You can change the address for the credit memo by replacing some portion of the usual billing address. Typically, you should use the same address for the credit memo that you use for the original invoice or invoices.

7. **(Optional . . . sort of) Provide the purchase order (PO) number.**

   If the credit memo adjusts the total remaining balance on a customer purchase order, you should probably enter the number of the purchase order into the P.O. No. text box.

8. **If the customer returns items, describe each item.**

   Move the cursor to the first row of the Item/ Description/Qty/Rate/Amount/Tax text box. In the first empty row of the box, activate the Item drop-down list and then select the item. After you select it, QuickBooks fills in the Description and Rate text boxes with whatever sales description and sales price you entered in the Item list. (You can edit this information if you want, but it isn't necessary.) Enter the number of items that the customer is returning (or not paying for) in the Qty text box. (After you enter this number, QuickBooks calculates the amount by multiplying Qty by Rate.) Enter each item that the customer is returning by filling in the empty rows of the list box.

In the case of inventory items, QuickBooks assumes that the items you're showing on a credit memo are returned to inventory. You want to adjust your inventory physical counts if unsold items are returned.

As with invoices, you can put as many items on a credit memo as you want. If you don't have enough room on a single page, QuickBooks keeps adding pages to the credit memo until you're finished. The total information, of course, goes on the last page.

9. **Describe any special items that the credit memo should include.**

If you want to issue a credit memo for other items that appear on the original invoice — freight, discounts, other charges, and so on — add descriptions of each item to the Item list.

To add descriptions of these items, activate the Item drop-down list of the next empty row and then select the special item. (You activate the list by clicking the field once to turn it into a drop-down list and then by clicking the field's down arrow to access the list box.) After QuickBooks fills in the Description and Rate text boxes, edit this information (if necessary). Enter each special item — subtotal, discount, freight, and so on — that you're itemizing on the credit memo.

If you want to include a Discount item, you need to stick a Subtotal item on the credit memo after the inventory or other items that you've discounted. Then stick a Discount item directly after the Subtotal item. In this way, QuickBooks calculates the discount as a percentage of the subtotal.

10. **(Optional) Add a customer message.**

Activate the Customer Message list and select a clever customer message.

11. Specify the sales tax.

Move the cursor to the Tax list box, activate the list box, and then select the correct sales tax.

12. (Optional, but a really good idea. . . .) Add a memo.

You can use the Memo text box to add a memo description to the credit memo. For example, you might use this description to explain your reasons for issuing the credit memo and to cross-reference the original invoice or invoices. Note that the Memo field prints on the Customer Statement. Figure 3-4 shows a completed Create Credit Memos/Refunds window.

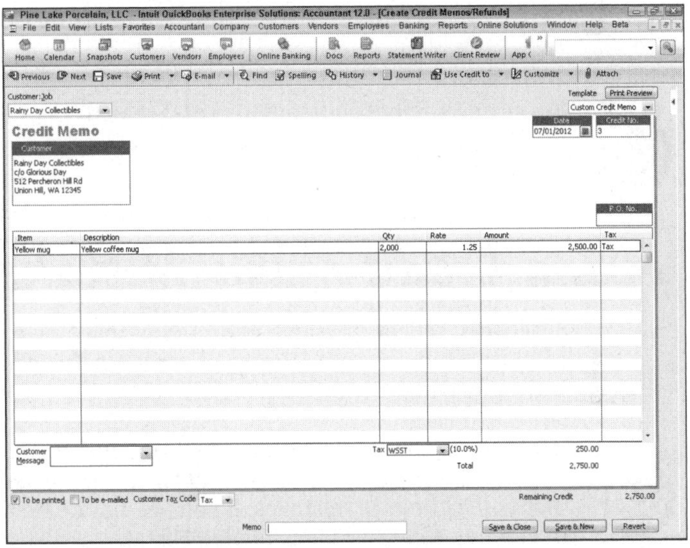

Figure 3-4: A completed Create Credit Memos/Refunds window.

13. If you want to delay printing this credit memo, clear the To Be Printed check box.

I want to postpone talking about what selecting the To Be Printed check box does until I finish the discussion of credit memo creation. Coverage of printing invoices and credit memos comes up in a later section.

14. Save the credit memo.

To save a completed credit memo, click either the
Save & New or Save & Close button. QuickBooks then
displays a dialog box that asks what you want to do
with the credit memo: Retain the credit, give a refund,
or apply the credit to an invoice. Make your choice by
clicking the button that corresponds to what you want
to do. If you choose Apply to Invoice, QuickBooks
asks for some additional information. QuickBooks
then saves the credit memo that's onscreen and, if
you clicked Save & New, displays an empty Create
Credit Memos/Refunds window so that you can create
another credit memo. (Note that you can page back
and forth through credit memos that you created
earlier by clicking the Next and the Previous buttons.)
When you're done creating credit memos, you can
click the credit memo form's Close button.

If you indicate that you want to print a refund check, QuickBooks
displays the Write Checks window and automatically fills out the
check, linking it to the memo.

Fixing Credit Memo Mistakes

Sure, I can repeat the same information that I gave you in the
section "Fixing Invoice Mistakes," earlier in this chapter, and
leave you with a strange feeling of *déjà vu.* But I won't.

Here's everything you need to know about fixing credit memo
mistakes: You can fix credit memo mistakes the same way
that you fix invoice mistakes. If you need more help, refer to
the earlier section "Fixing Invoice Mistakes."

History Lessons

Would you mind doing a small favor for me? Take another
peek at the images shown in Figures 3-1 and 3-4, and then look
at the Create Invoices window shown in Figure 3-5. See the difference? That panel of customer history information?

QuickBooks lets you add and remove historical information
about a customer from the Create Invoices window, the Create
Credit Memos/Refunds window, and most other "customer

information" windows, too. To add historical information about a customer to a window, click the Show History button that appears in the upper-right corner of the window just to the right of the Print Preview button. Note that you click links in the historical information panel to drill down and get more information about, for example, a listed transaction.

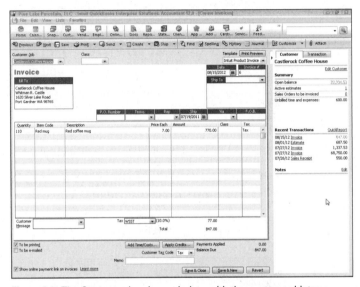

Figure 3-5: The Customer Invoices window with the customer history information.

Printing Invoices and Credit Memos

As part of setting up QuickBooks, you selected an invoice type. I assume that you have the raw paper stock for whatever invoice type you chose. If you're going to print on blank letterhead, for example, I assume that you have letterhead lying around. If you decide to use preprinted forms, I assume that you've ordered those forms and have received them.

I also assume that you've already set up your printer. If you've ever printed anything, your printer is already set up. Really.

Loading the forms into the printer

This part is easy. Simply load the invoice forms into the printer the same way you always load paper. Because you have one of about a jillion different printers, I can't give you the precise steps that you need to take, but if you've used a printer a bit, you should have no problem.

Setting up the invoice printer

You need to set up the invoice printer only once, but you need to specify a handful of general invoice-printing rules. These rules also apply to credit memos and purchase orders, by the way.

To set up your printer for invoice printing, follow these steps:

1. **Choose File⇨Printer Setup. From the Form Name drop-down list, choose Invoice.**

   QuickBooks displays the Printer Setup dialog box, as shown in Figure 3-6.

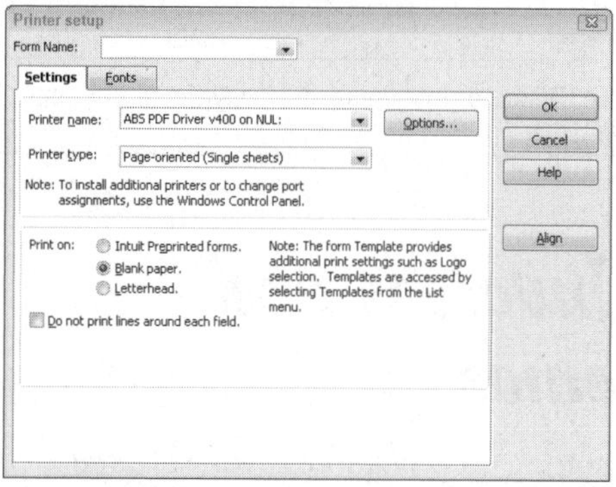

Figure 3-6: The Printer Setup dialog box.

2. **Select the printer that you want to use to print invoices.**

   Activate the Printer Name drop-down list to see the installed printers. Select the one that you want to use for printing invoices and purchase orders.

3. (Optional) Select the printer type.

The Printer Type drop-down list describes the kind of paper that your printer uses. You have two choices:

- *Continuous:* Your paper comes as one connected ream with perforated edges.

- *Page-Oriented:* Your paper is in single sheets.

4. Select the type of invoice form.

Select the option button that describes the type of form that you want to print on: Intuit Preprinted Forms, Blank Paper, or Letterhead. Then select the Do Not Print Lines around Each Field check box if you don't like the nice little boxes that QuickBooks creates to separate each field.

5. (Optional, but a really good idea . . .) Print a test invoice on real invoice paper.

Click the Align button. When QuickBooks displays the Align Printer dialog box, choose the type of invoice that you want to print from the list and then click OK. When QuickBooks displays the Fine Alignment dialog box, as shown in Figure 3-7, click the Print Sample button to tell QuickBooks to print a dummy invoice on whatever paper you've loaded in the invoice printer.

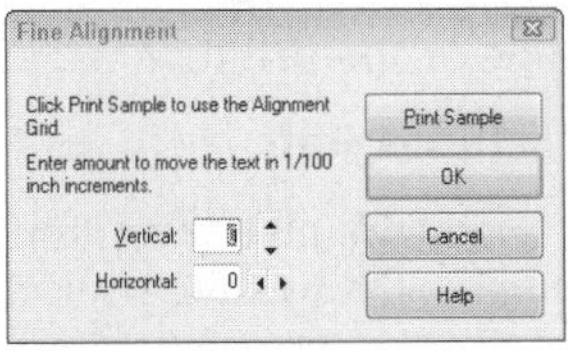

Figure 3-7: The Fine Alignment dialog box.

The dummy invoice that QuickBooks prints gives you a chance to see what your invoices will look like. The invoice also has a set of alignment gridlines that prints over the Bill To text box. You can use these gridlines if you need to fine-align your printer.

6. Fix any form-alignment problems.

If you see any alignment problems after you complete Step 5, you need to fix them. (Alignment problems usually occur only with impact printers. With laser printers or inkjet printers, sheets of paper feed into the printer the same way every time, so you almost never need to fiddle with the form alignment.)

To fix any big alignment problems — like stuff printing in the wrong place — you need to adjust how the paper feeds into the printer. When you finally get the paper loaded as best you can, be sure to note exactly how you have it loaded. You need to have the printer and paper set up the same way every time you print.

For minor (but nonetheless annoying) alignment problems, use the Fine Alignment dialog box's Vertical and Horizontal boxes to adjust the form's alignment. Then print another sample invoice. Go ahead and experiment a bit. You need to fine-tune the printing of the invoice form only once. Click OK in the Fine Alignment dialog box when you finish, and QuickBooks redisplays the Printer Setup dialog box.

Clicking the Options button in the Printer Setup dialog box (refer to Figure 3-6) opens the selected printer's Windows printer setup information, where you can do such things as specify quality settings or print order. Because this information relates to Windows and not to QuickBooks, I'm not going to explain it. If you're the curious type or accidentally click it and then have questions about what you see, refer either to your Windows user's guide or the printer's user's guide.

7. **Save your printer settings stuff.**

   After you finish fiddling with all the Printer Setup dialog box settings, click OK to save your changes.

   If you always want to use some particular settings to print a particular form (maybe you always print two copies of an invoice, for example), see the "Customizing Your Invoices and Credit Memos" section, later in this chapter.

You can print invoices and credit memos one at a time or in a batch. How you print them makes no difference to QuickBooks or to me, your humble author. Pick whatever way seems to fit your style the best. The following sections show you how.

Printing invoices and credit memos as you create them

If you want to print invoices and credit memos as you create them, follow these steps:

1. **Click the Print button after you create the invoice or credit memo.**

   After you fill in the boxes in the Create Invoices window (refer to Figure 3-2) or the Create Credit Memos/Refunds window (refer to Figure 3-4), click the Print button. QuickBooks, ever the faithful servant, displays either the Print One Invoice dialog box (as shown in Figure 3-8) or the Print One Credit Memo/ Refund dialog box (which looks almost like the Print One Invoice dialog box).

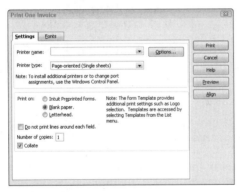

Figure 3-8: The Print One Invoice dialog box.

2. **(Optional) Select the type of invoice or credit memo form.**

   If you're using a different type of invoice or credit memo form than you've described for the invoice printer setup, select the type of form that you want to print from the Print On radio button choices. You can select Intuit Preprinted Forms, Blank Paper, or Letterhead.

   You shouldn't have to worry about printing test invoice or credit memo forms or fiddling with form alignment problems if you addressed these issues when you set up the invoice printer, so I'm not going to talk about the Align button here. If you want to do this kind of stuff and you need help, refer to the preceding section, "Setting up the invoice printer," in which I describe how to print test forms and fix form-alignment problems.

3. Print the form.

Click the Print button to send the form to the printer. QuickBooks prints the form.

4. Review the invoice or credit memo and reprint the form, if necessary.

Review the invoice or credit memo to see whether QuickBooks printed it correctly. If the form looks wrong, fix whatever caused the problem (perhaps you printed it on the wrong paper, for example) and reprint the form by clicking the Print button again.

Printing invoices in a batch

If you want to print invoices in a batch, you need to mark the To Be Printed check box that appears in the lower-left corner of the Create Invoices window. This check mark tells QuickBooks to put a copy of the invoice on a special invoices-to-be-printed list.

When you later want to print the invoices-to-be-printed list, follow these steps:

1. Display the Create Invoices window (choose Customers⇨Create Invoices), click the arrow next to the Print button, and choose Print Batch from the drop-down list.

QuickBooks displays the Select Invoices to Print dialog box, as shown in Figure 3-9. This box lists all the invoices that you marked as To Be Printed that you haven't yet printed.

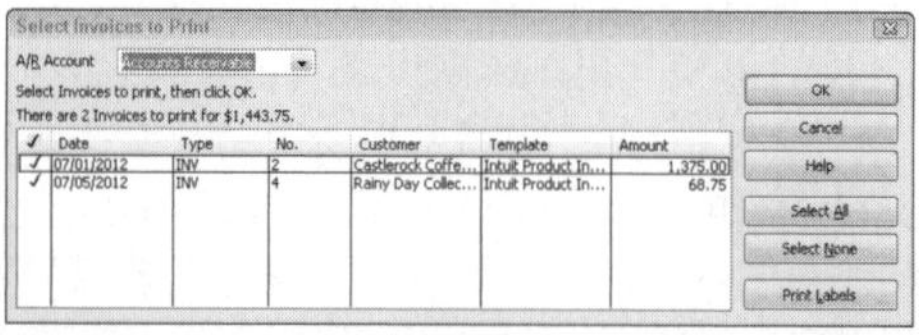

Figure 3-9: The Select Invoices to Print dialog box.

2. **Select the invoices that you want to print.**

   Initially, QuickBooks marks all the invoices with a check mark, indicating that they'll be printed. You can select and deselect individual invoices on the list by clicking them. You also can click the Select All button (to mark all the invoices) or the Select None button (to deselect all the invoices).

3. **Click OK.**

   After you correctly mark all the invoices you want to print — and none of the ones you don't want to print — click OK. QuickBooks displays the Print Invoices dialog box, as shown in Figure 3-10.

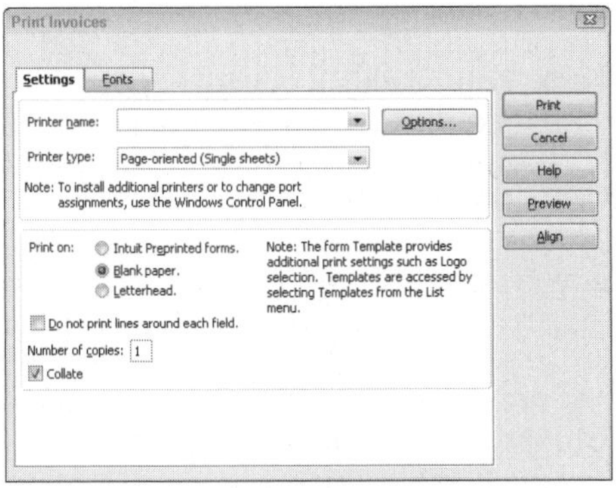

Figure 3-10: The Print Invoices dialog box.

4. **(Optional) Select the type of invoice form.**

   If you use a different type of invoice form than you described during the invoice setup, select the type of form that you want to print on by using the Print On options. You can choose Intuit Preprinted Forms, Blank Paper, or Letterhead.

5. **Print the forms.**

   Click the Print button to send the selected invoice forms to the printer. QuickBooks prints the forms and then displays a message box that asks whether the forms printed correctly.

6. **Review the invoice forms and reprint them if necessary.**

   Review the invoices to see whether QuickBooks printed them all correctly. If all the forms look okay, click OK in the message box. If one or more forms don't look okay, enter the invoice number of the first incorrect form in the message box. Then fix whatever problem fouled up the form (perhaps you printed it on the wrong paper, for example) and reprint the bad form(s) by clicking the Print button again. (The Print button is in the Print Invoices dialog box.)

Printing credit memos in a batch

If you want to print credit memos in a batch, you need to select the To Be Printed check box that appears in the lower-left corner of the Create Credit Memos/Refunds window. Selecting this box tells QuickBooks to put a copy of the credit memo on a special credit memos to-be-printed list.

Printing credit memos in a batch works similarly to printing invoices in a batch. Because I describe how to print invoices in a batch in the preceding section, here I speed through a description of printing credit memos in a batch. If you get lost or have questions, refer to the preceding section.

When you're ready to print the credit memos that are on the to-be-printed list, follow these steps:

1. **Display the Create Credit Memos/Refunds window (refer to Figure 3-4), click the down arrow next to the Print button, and choose Print Batch from the drop-down list.**

   QuickBooks displays the Select Credit Memos to Print dialog box.

2. **Select the credit memos that you want to print.**

3. **Click OK to display the Print Credit Memos dialog box.**

4. **Use the Print Credit Memos dialog box to describe how you want your credit memos to be printed.**

5. **Click the Print button to send the selected credit memos to the printer.**

   QuickBooks prints the credit memos.

Sending Invoices and Credit Memos via E-Mail

If you have e-mail already set up on your computer, you can e-mail invoices rather than print them. To e-mail an invoice or credit memo, click the Send button, which appears at the top of the Create Invoices window. (The button shows a picture of a little envelope with a green arrow.) QuickBooks displays the Send Invoice dialog box, as shown in Figure 3-11.

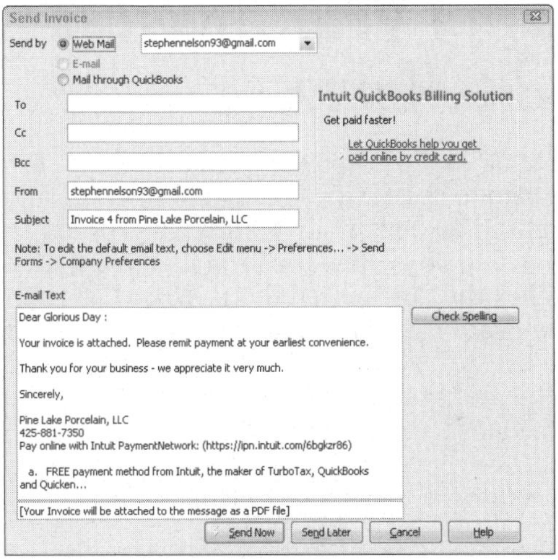

Figure 3-11: The Send Invoice dialog box.

To send your invoice via e-mail, enter the e-mail address of the business that you want to bill or refund money to, edit the message as appropriate (make sure to click that Check Spelling button), and then click the Send Now button.

If you want to wait to send your invoice, click the Send Later button while in the Send Invoice dialog box or select the To Be E-Mailed check box in the lower-left corner of the invoice window, and QuickBooks batches your e-mail invoices. You can send the entire batch later by clicking the arrow next to the Send button and choosing the Send Batch command. Note that QuickBooks also has a mailing service that you can sign up for. To get the dirt on this option, click the Send button and choose the Mail Invoice command from the menu that QuickBooks displays.

You can also fax invoices and credit memos from inside QuickBooks if you have a modem installed. To do this, click the Print button at the top of the Create Invoices or the Create Credit Memos/Refunds window, choose your fax/modem from the Printer Name drop-down list, and then use the wizard that appears to send the fax via your modem. (Long-distance charges may apply.)

Customizing Your Invoices and Credit Memos

With QuickBooks, you can easily customize the invoice and credit memo templates, or create new invoices and credit memos based on one of the existing QuickBooks templates. All you have to do is open the form that you want to customize and click the Customize button. When QuickBooks displays the Customize Your QuickBooks Forms window, you can click the Create New Design button to go to an Intuit web page that walks you through the steps to creating your own highly customized form (see Figure 3-12).

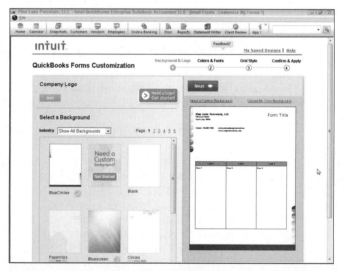

Figure 3-12: The Create New Design web page.

Alternatively, you can click the Customize Data Layout button (also available from the Customize Your QuickBooks Forms window) to display dialog boxes that supply buttons and boxes that you can use to first create a copy of the standard QuickBooks invoice or credit memo form and then modify the data that appears on the new copy of the form. Note that the customization dialog boxes provide a Preview area that shows what the customizations look like, so go hog-wild and be adventurous. (If you make a mess, just click Cancel to abandon your customization changes. Then, if you want, restart the process — perhaps a bit wiser and smarter for the experience.)

If you're creating a new invoice form using the customization dialog boxes, you can also click the Layout Designer button in the customization dialog box to open the Layout Designer window, as shown in Figure 3-13. In this window, you can become a true layout artist and observe how the overall look of your invoice changes when you move fields around the page with your mouse.

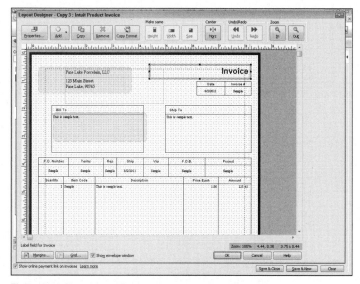

Figure 3-13: Use Layout Designer to customize an invoice.

Chapter 4

Reeling In the Dough

● ●

In This Chapter

▶ Recording and printing sales receipts

▶ Discovering special tips for retailers

▶ Fixing sales receipt mistakes

▶ Recording customer payments

▶ Correcting mistakes in recording customer payments

▶ Making deposits

▶ Tracking customer open invoices and collections

▶ Assessing finance charges

● ●

*Y*ou need to record the amounts that customers pay you when they fork over cash, at the time of a sale or after you invoice them. In this chapter, I describe how to record these payments and explain how to make bank deposits, track the amounts that customers owe and pay, and assess finance charges.

 If you've been using QuickBooks to prepare customer invoices, you're ready to begin recording payments. You'll have no problem. If you haven't been invoicing customers, you need to make sure that you have a couple of things ready to go before you can record cash sales.

First, you need to make sure that your lists are up-to-date. (I describe updating these lists in Chapter 2.) And second, if you want to print sales receipts, you need to have your printer set up to print them. You do so by choosing File⇨Printer Setup and then selecting Sales Receipt from the Form Name drop-down list. Setting up your printer to print sales receipts works just like setting it up to print invoices and credit memos (as I describe in Chapter 3).

Recording a Sales Receipt

You record a *sales receipt* when a customer pays you in full for the goods at the point of sale. Sales receipts work similarly to regular sales (for which you first invoice a customer and then later receive payment on the invoice). In fact, the big difference between the two types of sales is that sales receipts are recorded in a way that changes your cash balance rather than your accounts receivable balance.

In the following steps, I describe how to record sales receipts for products, which are the most complicated type of cash sale. Recording sales receipts for services works basically the same way, however. You simply fill in fewer fields.

1. **Choose Customers⇨Enter Sales Receipt.**

   Or, on the Home screen, click the Create Sales Receipts icon. Or, in the Customer Center, choose the customer from the list and then choose New Transactions⇨Sales Receipts. The Sales Receipt Template appears.

   The Enter Sales Receipts window appears, as shown in Figure 4-1.

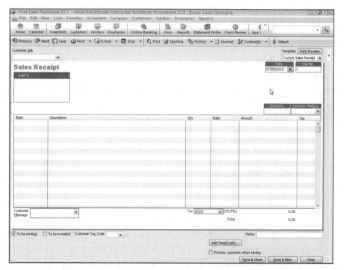

Figure 4-1: The Enter Sales Receipts window, strangely empty and perhaps a bit lonely.

Your Enter Sales Receipts window may not look exactly like mine for a couple of reasons. The first is that QuickBooks customizes (and you can customize) its forms to fit your particular type of business. The second reason is that QuickBooks may initially display a Payment toolbar on the sales receipt form and on the Receive Payment form. You can turn off the Payment toolbar by clicking its Close Toolbar button. You can turn on the Payment toolbar by choosing Edit⇨Preferences, selecting Sales & Customers, clicking My Preferences, and checking the Show Payment Toolbar box.

Customizing sales receipt forms works in a similar way to customizing invoices and credit memos, as I describe in Chapter 3. If your Enter Sales Receipts window includes more fields than I describe here, you can also turn to that chapter for help on how to fill out the additional fields or turn them off.

2. Identify the customer and, if necessary, the job.

Activate the Customer:Job drop-down list by clicking the down arrow to the right of the box. Scroll through the Customer:Job list until you see the customer or job name that you want and then click it. Note that unlike with invoices, the Customer:Job field isn't required for cash sales.

3. (Optional) Specify a class for the sales receipt.

If you're using classes to categorize transactions, activate the Class drop-down list and select the appropriate class for the sales receipt. (I don't show the Class list box in Figure 4-1, so don't look for it there.)

4. Date the sales receipt.

Press Tab to move the cursor to the Date text box. Then type the correct date in MM/DD/YYYY format. You can change the date by using any of the date-editing codes. (You can find these codes in Chapter 3 and on the online Cheat Sheet for this book at www. dummies.com/cheatsheet/quickbooks2012.)

5. (Optional) Enter a sale number.

QuickBooks suggests a cash sale number by adding 1 to the last cash sale number you used. Use this number or tab to the Sale No. text box and change the number to whatever you want.

6. Fix the Sold To address, if necessary.

QuickBooks grabs the billing address from the Customer list and uses the billing address as the Sold To address. You can change the address for the cash sale, however, by replacing the appropriate part of the usual billing address.

7. Record the check number.

Enter the customer's check number in the Check No. text box. If the customer is paying you with cold hard cash, you can leave the Check No. text box empty.

8. Specify the payment method.

To specify the payment method, activate the Payment Method drop-down list and select something from it: cash, check, Visa, MasterCard, or whatever. If you don't see the payment method that you want to use, you can add the method to the Payment Method list. Choose Add New to display the New Payment Method dialog box. Enter a description of the payment method in the text box and click OK.

9. Describe each item that you're selling.

Move the cursor to the first row of the Item/ Description/Qty/Rate/Amount/Tax list box. When you do, QuickBooks turns the Item field into a drop-down list. Activate the Item drop-down list of the first empty row in the list box and then select the item. When you do, QuickBooks fills in the Description and Rate text boxes with whatever sales description and sales price you entered in the Item list. (You can edit this information if you want, but that probably isn't necessary.) Enter the number of items sold in the Qty text box. Describe each of the other items you're selling by filling in the next empty rows of the list box.

If you add an inventory item to an invoice, QuickBooks adds a small button to the Quantity field when the cursor rests on the Quantity field. If you click the button, QuickBooks displays a window that describes the on-hand quantities of the inventory item.

If you've already read the chapter on invoicing customers (Chapter 3), what I'm about to tell you will seem very familiar: You can put as many items on a sales receipt as you want. If you don't have enough room on a single page, QuickBooks adds as many pages as you need to the receipt. The sales receipt total, of course, goes on the last page.

10. **Describe any special items that the sales receipt should include.**

    If you didn't set up the QuickBooks item file, you have no idea what I'm talking about. Here's the scoop: QuickBooks thinks that anything that you stick on a receipt (or an invoice, for that matter) is something that you're selling. If you sell blue, yellow, and red thingamajigs, you obviously need to add each of these items to the Item list. But if you add freight charges to your receipt, QuickBooks thinks that these charges are just another thingamajig and requires you to enter another item in the list. The same is true for a volume discount that you want to stick on the receipt. And if you add sales tax to your receipt, well, guess what? QuickBooks thinks that the sales tax is just another item that needs to be included in the Item list. (For more information about working with your Item list and adding new items, refer to Chapter 2.)

    To include one of these special items, move the cursor to the next empty row in the Item box, activate the drop-down list by clicking the arrow on the right side of the box, and then select the special item. After QuickBooks fills in the Description and Rate text boxes, you might need to edit this information. Enter each special item — subtotals, discounts, freight, and so on — that you're itemizing on the receipt by filling in the next empty row of the list box.

    If you selected the Taxable check box when you added the item to the Item list, the word _Tax_ appears in the Tax column to indicate that the item will be taxed.

    If you want to include a discount item (so that all the listed items are discounted), you need to stick a subtotal item on the receipt after the inventory items or other items you want to discount. Then stick the discount item directly after the subtotal item. In this way, QuickBooks calculates the discount as a percentage of the subtotal.

11. (Optional) Add a customer message.

Click in the Customer Message box, activate its drop-down list, and choose a clever customer message. To add customer messages to the customer message list, select Add New. When QuickBooks displays the New Customer Message box, fill it in and then click OK.

12. Specify the sales tax.

If you specify tax information when you create your company file during the QuickBooks Setup — remember how QuickBooks asked whether you charge sales tax? — QuickBooks fills in the default tax information by adding the taxable items (which are indicated by the word *Tax* in the Tax column) and multiplying by the percentage you indicated when you created your company file. If the information is okay, move on to Step 13. If not, move the cursor to the Tax box that's to the right of the Customer Message box, activate the drop-down list, and choose the correct sales tax. For more information about setting a default sales tax for a customer on the Customer list, read Chapter 2.

13. (Truly optional and probably unnecessary for cash sales) Add a memo in the Memo text box.

You can include a memo description with the cash sale information. This memo isn't for your customer. It doesn't even print on the cash receipt, should you decide to print one. The memo is for your eyes only. Memo descriptions give you a way to store information that's related to a sale with the sales receipt information.

14. Decide whether you're going to print the receipt.

If you aren't going to print the receipt, make sure that the To Be Printed check box is empty — if not, click it to remove the check.

Figure 4-2 shows a completed Enter Sales Receipts window.

15. Save the sales receipt.

To save a completed sales receipt, click either the Save & Close button or the Save & New button. QuickBooks saves the sales receipt that's onscreen and then, if you clicked Save & New, displays an empty Enter Sales Receipts window so that you can create another sales receipt. (Note that you can page back and forth through receipts that you created earlier by clicking the Next and Previous buttons and display and remove historical information for the selected customer by clicking the Show History button. The Show History button is the little arrow to the right of the Print Preview button in the upper-right corner of the screen.) When you're done creating sales receipts, you can click the Enter Sales Receipts window's Close button.

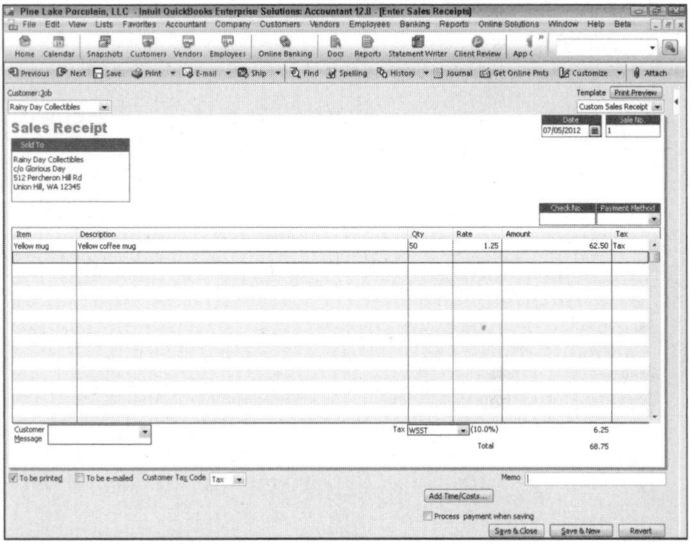

Figure 4-2: The completed Enter Sales Receipts window.

Printing a Sales Receipt

To print a single sales receipt as you're recording the information, click the Print button in the Enter Sales Receipts window. The Print One Sales Receipt dialog box appears, as shown in Figure 4-3. The following steps tell you how to complete this dialog box:

Print One Sales Receipt

Settings | Fonts

Printer name: [▼]   Options...

Printer type: [Page-oriented (Single sheets)   ▼]

Note: To install additional printers or to change port
assignments, use the Windows Control Panel.

Print on: ○ Intuit Preprinted Forms.
● Blank paper.
○ Letterhead.

Note: The form Template provides
additional print settings such as Logo
selection. Templates are accessed by
selecting Templates from the List
menu.

☐ Do not print lines around each field.

Number of copies: [1]

☑ Collate

[Print]
[Cancel]
[Help]
[Preview]
[Align]

Figure 4-3: The Print One Sales Receipt dialog box.

1. **Select the type of sales receipt form.**

   If you're using a different sales receipt form type than
   you described for the invoice/purchase order (PO)
   printer setup, select the type of form that you want
   to print on by selecting a radio button in the Print
   On section. You can choose Intuit Preprinted Forms,
   Blank Paper, or Letterhead. (See Chapter 3 for more
   on these printer options.)

   You shouldn't have to worry about printing test
   receipts or fiddling with form alignment problems if
   you addressed these issues during the invoice/PO
   printer setup, so I'm not going to talk about the Align
   button here. If you want to print a test receipt or need
   to change the alignment, read Chapter 3 for how to
   proceed.

2. **Print that puppy!**

   Click the Print button to send the form to the printer.
   QuickBooks prints the sales receipt.

3. **Review the sales receipt and reprint the form, if
   necessary.**

   Review the sales receipt to see whether QuickBooks
   printed it correctly. If the form doesn't look okay, fix
   whatever problem fouled up the printing; perhaps you
   forgot to include the company name and address, for
   example. Then reprint the form by clicking the Print
   button (in the Enter Sales Receipts window) again,
   selecting the form on which you want to print (again),

and then clicking the Print button in the Print One
Sales Receipt dialog box (you got it — again).

To print a batch of receipts, make sure that you select the To
Be Printed check box on each receipt that you want to print
and then display the Enter Sales Receipts window, click the
arrow beside the Print button, and choose Print Batch from
the drop-down list. QuickBooks displays the Select Receipts
to Print dialog box, which enables you to choose which
receipts to print. Select the desired receipts by putting a
check mark in the first column and then click OK. The Print
Sales Receipts dialog box appears. This dialog box resembles
the Print One Sales Receipt dialog box in just about every
way, and the instructions work in exactly the same manner.
For help with this dialog box, refer to the sections on printing
invoices and credit memos in batches in Chapter 3.

Special Tips for Retailers

Are you a retailer? If so, you're probably saying, "Hey, idiot,
what you just described is way too much work to do every
time someone walks into the store and buys some $3 item."

You know what? You're right. So here's what retailers do to
record their sales. Retailers record the day's sales by using
one, two, or three sales receipt transactions. Retailers don't
record each individual sales receipt transaction.

Say that some coffee mug retailer sold 2,500 red coffee mugs for
the day for $3.50 each. In that case, at the end of the day, the
retailer needs to record total sales of $8,750 and then the sales
tax. (In my example here, sales tax is 9.5 percent.) With these
example numbers, the *daily* sales would be recorded using a
sales receipt transaction like the one shown earlier in Figure 4-2.

Pretty straightforward, right? And that's not too much work,
all things considered.

Let me share a handful of other tips for recording retail sales:

> ✔ **You probably want to record a sales receipt transac-
> tion for each deposit you make.** In this manner, you can
> indicate that a particular sales receipt transaction (really

a batch of sales) is deposited at one time into your bank account — which makes reconciling your bank account relatively easy.

✔ **You probably want to separate cash sales from credit card sales because often credit card sales are handled differently.** Your credit card processing company, for example, might hold on to credit card sales for a few days, or it might deduct a fee before depositing the money into your bank account. You want to record a separate sales receipt transaction for each deposit that you make (or some other company makes) into the bank account — again, to make reconciling the bank account easier.

✔ **If you don't use the Item list to monitor your inventory (because you have way too many items to store in the QuickBooks Item list), use items that are designated as non-inventory parts.** For example, you might use non-inventory part items, such as *daily cash sales, daily AmEx sales,* and *daily Visa/MC sales* if you make three deposits every day for cash and check sales, for American Express sales, and for Visa and MasterCard sales. If you don't track inventory in your items file, your CPA handles the inventory and cost of goods sold calculations on your tax return. He or she probably also records a journal entry transaction to get your account balances correct as of the end of your fiscal year.

✔ **You may want to look at the QuickBooks Point of Sale system.** The QuickBooks Point of Sale system makes it easy to quickly record cash register sales. In fact, the more expensive version of the QuickBooks Point of Sale system comes with a scanner, a receipt printer, and a cash drawer. When you ring up a sale with the QuickBooks Point of Sale system, the software automatically records your sales and the effect on inventory and cost of goods sold.

✔ **You also may not want to use inventory items to track your inventory if you're a retailer.** You may instead want to use non–inventory part items or generic non-inventory part items. In this way, QuickBooks won't track the quantity of items that sell — only the dollar amounts of your sales.

Correcting Sales Receipt Mistakes

If you make a mistake in entering a sales receipt (cash sale), don't worry. Here's a list of common problems and how to fix them:

- **If the sales receipt is still displayed onscreen:** If the sales receipt is still onscreen, you can move the cursor to the box or button that's incorrect and then fix the mistake. Most of the bits of information that you enter in the Enter Sales Receipts window are fairly short or are entries that you've selected from a list. You can usually replace the contents of some field by typing over whatever's already there or by making a couple of quick clicks. If you really messed up and want to start over from scratch, you can click the Clear button. To save a receipt after you've entered it correctly, click either the Save & Close button or the Save & New button.

If you need to insert a line in the middle of a sales receipt, right-click where you want to insert the line and choose Insert Line from the shortcut menu. To delete a line, right-click it and then choose Delete Line from the shortcut menu.

- **If the sales receipt isn't displayed onscreen:** If the sales receipt isn't onscreen, and you haven't yet printed it, you can use the Next and Previous buttons to page through the sales receipts. When you get to the one with the error, fix the error as I describe in the preceding bullet. If you make a mistake while editing a receipt, you can click the Revert button to go back to the saved receipt and not save your changes. Note that Clear toggles to Revert after you edit a transaction.

Even if you printed the customer's receipt, you can make the sort of change that I just described. For example, you can page through the sales receipts by using the Next and Previous buttons until you find the receipt (now printed) with the error. And you can correct the error and print the receipt again. I'm not so sure that you want to go this route, however. Things will be much cleaner if you void the cash sale by displaying the sales receipt and choosing Edit⇨Void Sales Receipt. Then enter a new, correct cash sales transaction.

✔ **If you don't want the sales receipt:** You usually won't want to delete sales receipts, but you can delete them. (You'll almost always be in much better shape if you just void the sales receipt.) To delete the receipt, display it in the Enter Sales Receipts window (choose Customers⇨Enter Sales Receipt and then page through the sales receipts by using the Next and Previous buttons until you see the cash sale that you want to delete) and then choose Edit⇨Delete Sales Receipt. When QuickBooks asks you to confirm the deletion, click Yes.

If you want to see a list of all your cash sales, choose Edit⇨Find, and the Simple Find screen appears. Select Transaction Type⇨Sales Receipt and then click Find. Select the receipt you want to see from the list that appears. If you're already viewing a sales receipt, choose Edit⇨Find Sales Receipts. When you click the Find button, another screen pops up and asks for details of the sales receipt that you're looking for. Click the Find button on that screen, and QuickBooks gives you a list of your cash sales for the criteria you selected.

Recording Customer Payments

If your customers don't always pay you upfront for their purchases, you need to record another type of payment: the payments that customers make to pay off or pay down what you've invoiced them. To record the payments, of course, you first need to record invoices for the customer. If you issue credit memos that customers can use to reduce the amounts they owe, you also first need to record credit memos for each customer. (Check out Chapter 3 to find out how to create and record these items.) The rest is easy.

To access a wealth of customer information all on one page, click the Customer Center icon at the top of the screen or choose Customers⇨Customer Center. The Customer Center appears, listing outstanding balances for all customers and detailed information for the customer selected in the Customers & Jobs list.

To display the Receive Payments window, click the Receive Payments icon on the Home screen or click the Customer Center icon and select the customer you need. Click New Transactions and Receive Payments or choose Customers⇨Receive Payments from the top menus. Then describe the customer payment and the invoices paid. If you want the gory details, read through the following steps:

1. **Choose Customers⇨Receive Payments.**

   The Receive Payments window appears, as shown in Figure 4-4.

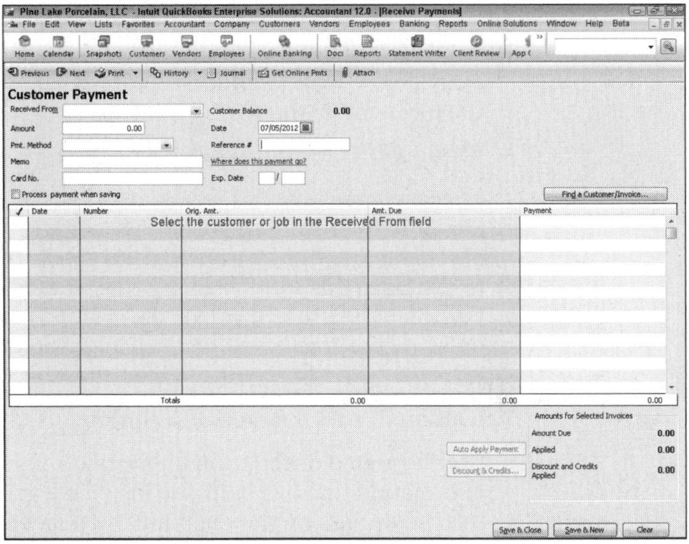

Figure 4-4: The Receive Payments window.

2. **Identify the customer and, if necessary, the job.**

   Activate the Received From drop-down list and select the customer (and job, if necessary) by clicking its name. QuickBooks lists the open, or unpaid, invoices for the customer in the list box at the bottom of the window.

3. **Specify the payment date.**

   Press Tab to move the cursor to the Date text box (the one right above the Reference # text box), and type the correct date in MM/DD/YYYY format. To edit the date, you can use the secret date-editing codes that I describe in Chapter 3 and on the online Cheat Sheet for this book at `www.dummies.com/cheatsheet/ quickbooks2012`.

4. **Enter the amount of the payment.**

   Move the cursor to the Amount field and type the customer payment amount. ***Note:*** If the customer is paying with a credit card and your merchant bank deducts a fee from the individual payments, record the full amount of the payment on this payment screen and the merchant fee later on the Deposit screen.

5. **(Optional) Specify the payment method.**

   Activate the Pmt. Method drop-down list and choose the payment method.

6. **(Optional) Enter the check number.**

   You can guess how this works, right? You move the cursor to the Reference # field. Then you type the check number from the customer's check. Do you need to complete this step? Nah. But this bit of information might be useful if you or the customer later ends up with questions about what checks paid for what invoices. So I'd go ahead and enter the check number.

7. **(Optional) Add a memo description.**

   Use the Memo description for storing some bit of information that will help you in some way. Note that this field prints on the Customer Statement.

8. **If the customer has any outstanding credits, decide whether to apply them in this payment.**

   QuickBooks totals the amounts of any of the customer's existing credits. They can be anything from an overpayment on a previous invoice to a return credit or anything else.

   When you create a new invoice, QuickBooks notifies you that there are credits available on the customer's account and asks whether you want to apply any of them to the new invoice.

   If you want to apply a credit memo to a specific open invoice, select the invoice and then click the

Discounts & Credits button. When QuickBooks displays the Credits tab of the Discount and Credits dialog box, as shown in Figure 4-5, click the credit memo that you want to apply and then click Done.

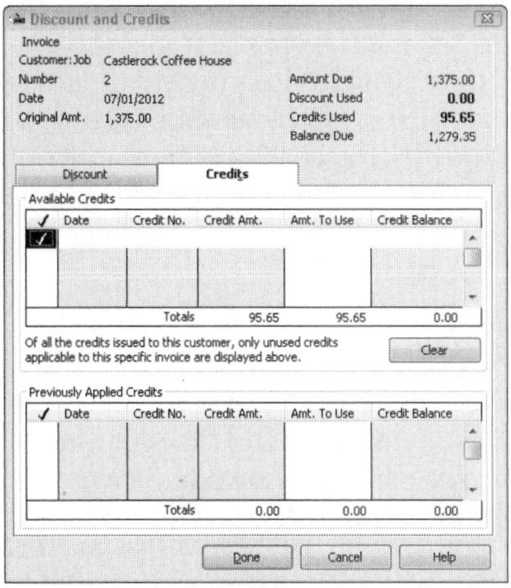

Figure 4-5: The Credits tab of the Discount and Credits dialog box.

9. **Identify which open invoices the customer is paying.**

By default, QuickBooks automatically applies the payment to the open invoices, starting with the oldest open invoice. You can change this application by entering amounts in the Payment column. Simply click the open invoice's payment amount and enter the correct amount.

You can leave a portion of the payment unapplied, if you want to. QuickBooks then asks what you want to do with the overpayment: You can leave the amount on account to be applied or refund the amount to the customer or client. By the way, if you record an underpayment, QuickBooks asks whether you want to just leave the unpaid amount sitting there or want to instead write off the remaining balance.

If you want to apply the customer payment to the oldest open invoices, click the Auto Apply Payment button. If you want to unapply payments that you already applied to open invoices, click the Clear Selections button. Clear Selections and Auto Apply

Payment are the same button. QuickBooks changes the name of the button, depending on whether you already applied payments.

10. **Adjust the early payment or other discounts, if necessary.**

If you offer payment terms that include an early pay-ment discount, QuickBooks automatically reduces the open invoice original amount (shown in the Orig. Amt. column) by the early payment discount that you specify to calculate the adjusted amount due (shown in the Amt. Due column) if the payment is dated within the discount period.

To specify any other discounts, select the open invoice that you want to adjust. Then click the Discount & Credits button. With little or no hesita-tion, the Discount tab of the Discount and Credits dialog box appears, as shown in Figure 4-6. Type the dollar amount of the discount in the Amount of Discount text box. Then specify the expense account that you want to use to track discounts by activating the Discount Account drop-down list and selecting one of the accounts. (Interest Expense is probably a good account to use unless you want to set up a spe-cial expense account called something like *Discount Expense* or *Discounts Given.*)

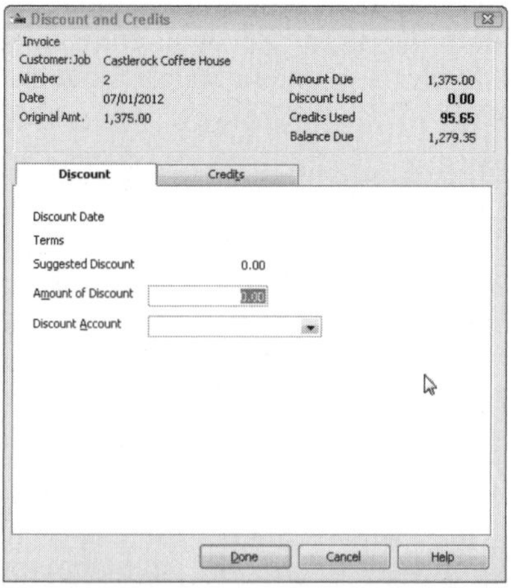

Figure 4-6: The Discount tab of the Discount and Credits dialog box.

When you're finished, click Done to return to the Receive Payments window.

11. **Record the customer payment information.**

After you identify which invoices the customer is paying — the unapplied amount should probably show as zero — you're ready to record the customer payment information. You can do so by clicking either the Save & New button or the Save & Close button. QuickBooks saves the customer payment shown onscreen. If you click Save & New, QuickBooks displays an empty Receive Payments window so that you can enter another payment.

You can return to customer payments you recorded earlier by clicking the Previous button.

Correcting Mistakes in Customer Payments Entries

You can correct mistakes that you make in entering customer payments in basically the same way that you correct mistakes that you make in entering cash sales.

First, you display the window you used to enter the transaction. In the case of customer payments, click the Customer Center icon and select the customer you need. You see a list of that customer's transactions on the right side. Double-click the payment transaction you want to change, and the original payments screen appears. And then you make your changes. Then you click Save & Close. Pretty straightforward, right?

If you already recorded a deposit that includes the payment you want to delete or edit, you need to delete the deposit before you can delete or edit the payment.

Making Bank Deposits

Whenever you record a cash sale or a customer payment on an invoice, QuickBooks adds the cash to its list of undeposited funds. These undeposited funds could be a bunch of checks that you haven't yet deposited, or they could consist of *coinage* (currency and coins) or even credit card payments, if you accept those.

You can also tell QuickBooks to give you the choice of indicating that a particular payment or sales receipt is deposited directly into a specified account. To tell QuickBooks to give you this choice, choose Edit⇨Preferences, scroll down to the Payments icon, click the Company Preferences tab, and then deselect the Use Undeposited Funds as a Default Deposit to Account option. After you make this change, QuickBooks adds buttons and a box to the lower-left corner of the Enter Sales Receipt and Receive Payment windows so that you can indicate into which bank account the money is deposited.

Eventually, though, you'll want to take the money out from under your mattress and deposit it in the bank. To do so, follow these steps:

1. **Choose Banking⇨Make Deposits.**

   Alternatively, select Record Deposits on the Home screen in the Banking section.

   The Payments to Deposit dialog box appears, as shown in Figure 4-7. This dialog box initially lists all the payments, regardless of the payment method. You can, however, use the View Payment Method Type drop-down list to indicate that you want to see payments only of a particular type — such as credit card payments. (This feature can be pretty handy because it lets you batch all your credit card transactions together.)

2. **Select the payments that you want to deposit.**

   Click a payment or cash receipt to place a check mark in front of it, marking it for deposit. If you want to deselect a payment, click it again. To deselect all the payments, click the Select None button. To select all the payments, click the Select All button. If you have gobs of payments to look through, you can also filter the list by clicking View Payment Method Type at the top and see only the Cash or Credit Cards to select among. If you're recording credit card payments deposited, you don't need to sort through the check payments, also. They aren't gone; they just don't appear until you select that type of payment or All.

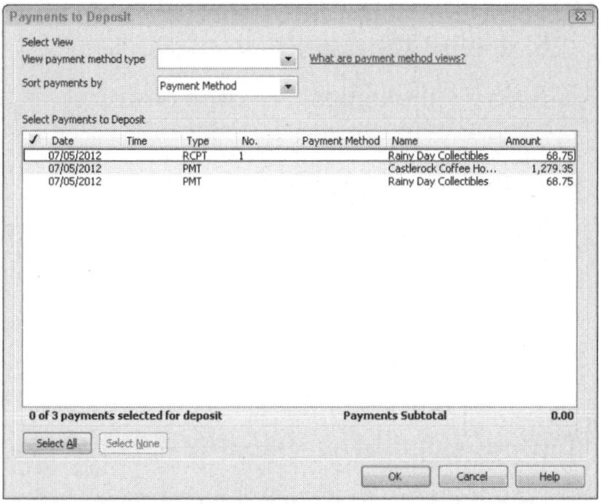

Figure 4-7: The Payments to Deposit dialog box.

3. Click OK.

After you indicate which payments you want to deposit, click OK. QuickBooks displays the Make Deposits window, as shown in Figure 4-8.

If you need to redisplay the Payments to Deposit dialog box — maybe you made a mistake or something, and now you need to go back and fix it — click the Payments button at the top of the Make Deposits screen. Note, though, that QuickBooks won't display the Payments to Deposit dialog box unless the undeposited funds list still has undeposited payments in it.

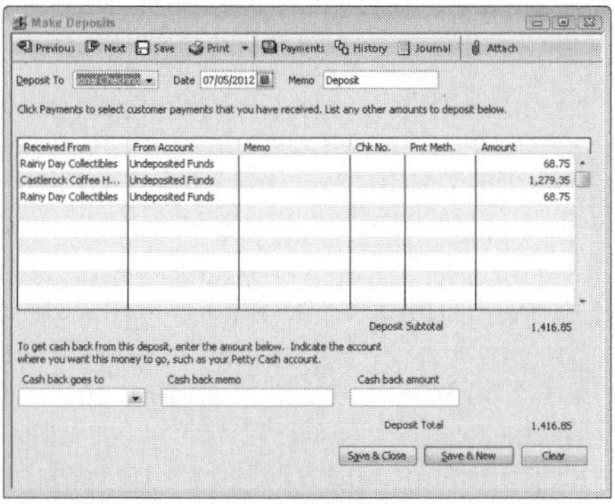

Figure 4-8: The Make Deposits window.

4. **Tell QuickBooks into which bank account you want to deposit the money.**

   Activate the Deposit To drop-down list and choose the bank account in which you want to place the funds.

5. **Specify the deposit date.**

   Press Tab to move the cursor to the Date text box and then type the correct date in MM/DD/YYYY format. Use the secret date-editing codes if you need to edit the date. (Get these codes from Chapter 3 or from the online Cheat Sheet at www.dummies.com/cheat sheet/quickbooks2012 if you don't know them.)

6. **(Optional) Add a memo description if you want to.**

   I don't know what sort of memo description you'd add for a deposit. Sorry. A bank deposit is a bank deposit. At least to me.

7. **Specify the cash-back amount.**

   If you want cash back from the deposit, activate the Cash Back Goes To drop-down list and choose a cash account, such as Petty Cash. Then enter a memo in the Cash Back Memo text box and the amount of cash back you're taking in the Cash Back Amount text box.

8. **Record the deposit by clicking the Save & Close button or the Save & New button.**

   If you click Save & New, QuickBooks displays a new blank Make Deposits window.

If you sometimes take cash from the register or from the day's collections to spend on business supplies, for COD (collect on delivery) payments, and even for salaries, you enter the cash payment transaction as another transaction line in the Make Deposits window (refer to Figure 4-8). For example, if you use $50 from the cash register to pay for office supplies from Acme Office Store, you enter another line into the Make Deposits window. You enter **Acme Office Store** into the Received From column, your office supplies expense account into the From Account column, and **–50** into the Amount column. You use a *negative* amount to reduce the total deposit to the correct amount that is actually deposited into the checking account and to charge the expense account for the amount paid out. This is also where you record the

Merchant Fees deducted from your credit card deposits I mention earlier in this section.

Improving Your Cash Inflow

I'm not going to provide a lengthy discussion of how to go about collecting cash from your customers. I do, however, want to quickly tell you about a couple of other details. You need to know how to monitor what your customers owe you and how to assess finance charges. Don't worry, though. I explain these two things as briefly as I can.

Tracking what your customers owe

You can track what a customer owes in a couple of ways. Probably the simplest method is to display the Customer Center by choosing Customer⇨Customer Center. Next, select the customer from the Customers & Jobs list (which appears along the left edge of the window). QuickBooks whips up a page that lists transactions for the customer. It also shows the customer's contact information. Figure 4-9 shows the Customer Center information for a customer.

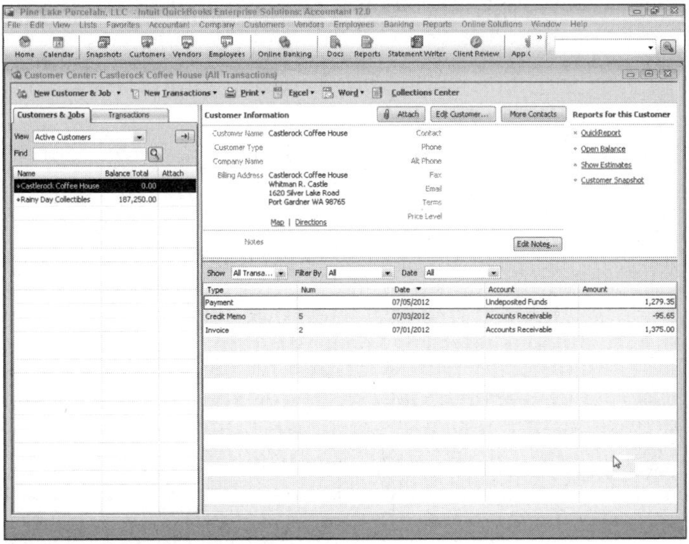

Figure 4-9: The Customer Center.

You also should be aware that QuickBooks provides several nifty accounts receivable (A/R) reports. You get to these reports by clicking the Report Center icon and choosing Customers & Receivables. Or you can choose Reports⇨Customers & Receivables. QuickBooks then displays a submenu of about a half-dozen reports that describe how much money customers owe you. Some reports, for example, organize open invoices into different groups based on how old the invoices are. (These reports are called *agings*.) Some reports summarize only invoices or payments. And some reports show each customer's open, or unpaid, balance.

In Chapter 6, I describe, in general terms, how you go about producing and printing QuickBooks reports. So read Chapter 6 if you have questions. Let me also say that you can't hurt anything or foul up your financial records just by printing reports. So go ahead and noodle around.

You can print a statement to send to a customer by choosing Customers⇨Create Statements. Use the Create Statements dialog box to describe which customers you want to print statements for and the date ranges you want the statements to show, and then click Print or E-Mail to print or e-mail the statements. Statements are a handy way to remind forgetful customers or clients about overdue amounts. You don't, by the way, need to send statements to everybody for every month. In my CPA practice, I send out statements a couple of times a year to clients with past-due accounts. This friendly reminder always produces a handful of quick payments and awkward apologies.

Assessing finance charges

I wasn't exactly sure where to stick this discussion of finance charges. Because finance charges seem to relate to collecting the cash your customers owe, I figure that I'm okay talking about assessing finance charges here.

QuickBooks assesses finance charges on unpaid open invoices without considering any unapplied payments. Accordingly, you'll want to make sure that you apply any payments and credit memos to open invoices before assessing finance charges.

To assess finance charges, follow these steps:

1. **Choose Edit⇨Preferences, click the Finance Charge icon in the list on the left, and then click the Company Preferences tab.**

   To be able to assess finance charges, you first need to set them up.

   Only the QuickBooks administrator can change the company finance charge settings, and he or she can do so only in single-user mode.

   QuickBooks displays the Preferences dialog box, as shown in Figure 4-10. (If you've assessed finance charges before, QuickBooks displays the Assess Finance Charges window. You can display the Preferences dialog box and check or edit your finance charge settings by clicking the Settings button in the Assess Finance Charges window.)

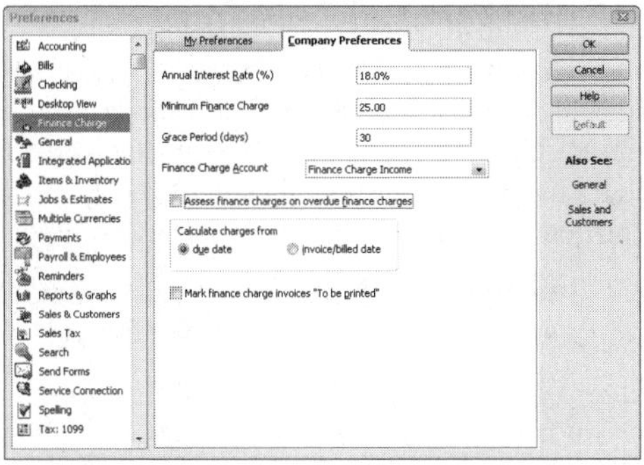

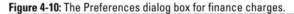

Figure 4-10: The Preferences dialog box for finance charges.

2. **Enter the annual interest rate that you want to use to calculate finance charges.**

   Move the cursor to the Annual Interest Rate (%) text box and enter the annual interest rate.

3. **(Optional) Enter the minimum finance charge — if one exists.**

   Move the cursor to the Minimum Finance Charge text box and enter the minimum charge. If you always

charge at least $25.00 on a past-due invoice, for exam-
ple, type **25**.

4. **Enter the number of days of grace that you give.**

    Days of Grace. That sounds kind of like an artsy movie
    or serious novel, doesn't it? Basically, this number is
    how many days of slack you're willing to cut people.
    If you type **30** in the Grace Period (Days) text box,
    QuickBooks doesn't start assessing finance charges
    until 30 days after the invoice is past due.

5. **Specify which account you want to use to track the
   finance charges.**

    Activate the Finance Charge Account drop-down list,
    and select an Income or Other Income type account.

6. **Indicate whether you want to charge finance charges
   on finance charges.**

    Does this statement make sense? If you charge some-
    body a finance charge, and he or she doesn't pay the
    finance charge, eventually it becomes past due, too. So
    then what do you do the next time you assess finance
    charges? Do you calculate a finance charge on the
    finance charge? If you want to do this — and if state and
    local laws permit you to — select the Assess Finance
    Charges on Overdue Finance Charges check box.

7. **Tell QuickBooks whether it should calculate finance
   charges from the due date or the invoice date.**

    Select either the Due Date or Invoice/Billed Date
    option button. As you might guess, you calculate
    bigger finance charges if you start accruing interest on
    the invoice date.

8. **Tell QuickBooks whether it should print finance
   charge invoices.**

    Select the check box for Mark Finance Charge Invoices
    "To Be Printed" if you want to print invoices later for
    the finance charges that you calculate.

9. **Click OK.**

    After you use the Preferences dialog box to tell
    QuickBooks how the finance charges should be calcu-
    lated, click OK.

10. **Choose Customers⇨Assess Finance Charges.**

    Alternatively, click the Finance Charges icon on the
    Home screen. The Assess Finance Charges window
    appears, as shown in Figure 4-11. This window shows
    all the finance charges that QuickBooks has calcu-
    lated, organized by customer.

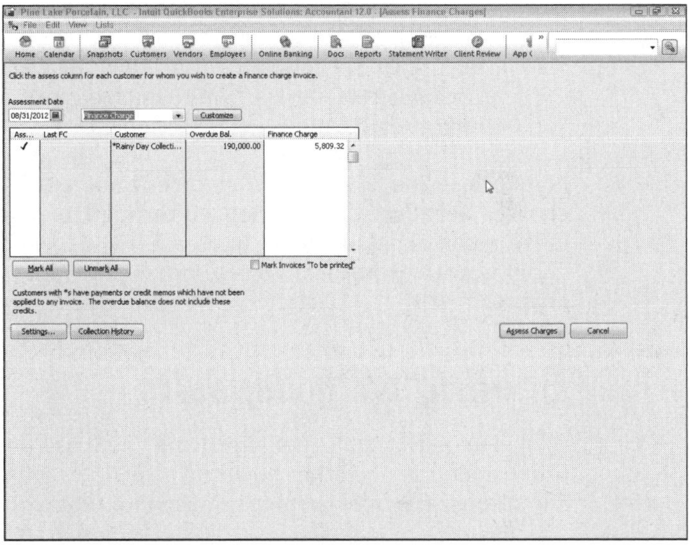

Figure 4-11: The Assess Finance Charges window.

11. **Give the finance charge assessment date.**

    Move the cursor to the Assessment Date text box
    and enter the date when you're assessing the finance
    charges, which I'm willing to bet is the current date.
    (This date is also the invoice date that will be used on
    the finance charge invoices, if you create them.)

12. **Confirm which customers you want to be assessed
    finance charges.**

    QuickBooks initially marks all the finance charges,
    which means that it sets up a new invoice for each
    finance charge. (QuickBooks marks finance charges
    with a little check mark.) If you want to unmark (or,
    later, mark) a finance charge, click it. To unmark all the

charges, click the Unmark All button. To mark all the charges, click the Mark All button.

You can produce a collections report for any of the customers or jobs listed in the Assess Finance Charges window by selecting the customer name and then clicking the Collection History button.

13. Click the Assess Charges button.

When the Assess Finance Charges window correctly describes the finance charges that you want to assess, click Assess Charges. You're finished with the finance charge calculations and assessments.

I don't describe how to print invoices that contain finance charges because I already slogged through invoice printing in painstaking detail in Chapter 3. If you have questions about how to print the invoices, you might want to visit that chapter.

Dealing with deposits

While I'm on the subject of improving your cash flow, let me briefly mention one other powerful cash flow technique — and discuss the bookkeeping required for that technique.

One easy way to improve your cash flow is to accept or require upfront deposits or retainers from clients or customers before you do the actual work. In other words, before you begin work or order inventory or do whatever is the first step in your business for completing a sale, you collect cold, hard cash.

Unfortunately, these *customer deposits,* as they're called, create a bit of bookkeeping trouble. The question becomes, basically, how do you record a check or cash deposit for stuff that you haven't yet done or sold? You have two basic options:

✔ **The Easy Way:** You can just record a sales receipt for the service or product. (See "Recording a Sales Receipt" at the beginning of this chapter.) In this way, you count the cash coming into your business. And you recognize the revenue. Note, too, that if the deposit is nonrefundable — and for cash flow

purposes, the deposit should be nonrefundable —
you should count the revenue when you receive the
deposit if you're a cash-basis taxpayer. (You probably
are a cash-basis taxpayer, but ask your tax advisor if
you aren't sure.)

✔ **The Precise Way:** You can recognize the deposit as a
new liability. You do this by creating a journal entry
that records the increase in your cash account and that
records the increase in your Customer Deposits current
liability account. If the deposit is refundable and you're
a cash-basis taxpayer, or if you're an accrual-basis taxpayer, you probably should use this method. When your
sale is completed and invoiced later, use the Customer
Deposit item as a minus amount on the sales invoice to
move the amount from the liability account and apply it
to the invoice balance due.

Chapter 5

Paying the Bills

• •

In This Chapter

▶ Using the Write Checks window to pay bills

▶ Using the accounts payable method to pay bills

▶ Deleting and editing bill payments

▶ Reminding yourself to pay bills

▶ Tracking vehicle mileage

▶ Paying sales tax

• •

*Q*uickBooks gives you two ways to pay and record your bills. And you have many options when it comes to deciding when to pay your bills, how to pay your bills, and how to record your bills for the purposes of tracking inventory and expenses.

In this chapter, I explain not only how to pay vendor bills but also how to pay that all-important bill that so many businesses owe to their state and local governments. I'm talking, of course, about sales tax.

Pay Now or Pay Later?

When it comes to paying bills, you have a fundamental choice to make. You can either record and pay your bills simultaneously, or record your bills as they come in but then pay them when they're due. The first method is easiest, as you might guess, because you do everything at once. The second method, called the *accounts payable method,* gives you more accurate financial records and makes for more precise management of your cash and outstanding bills.

If you have a small business with little overhead, you may just as well record and pay bills simultaneously. If you need precise measurement of your expenses and bills, though — if you want to use what's termed *accrual-basis accounting* — you should use the accounts payable method of paying bills. I should note, too, that using the accounts payable method with QuickBooks isn't as difficult as it may seem at first.

And now you're ready to begin. In the next section, I describe how to pay bills by writing checks. A little later in the chapter, in the "Recording Your Bills the Accounts Payable Way" section, you find out how to pay bills by using the accounts payable method.

Recording Your Bills by Writing Checks

When you record bills by writing checks, you're doing *cash-basis accounting*. In a nutshell, this means that you count bills as expenses when you write the check to pay the bill.

A trade-off is implicit in the choice to use cash-basis accounting. If you use cash-basis accounting — which is what I do in my little business — you greatly simplify your bookkeeping, but you lose precision in your measurement of your expenses. And you don't keep track of your unpaid bills inside QuickBooks. They just stack up in a pile next to your desk.

As long as you understand this trade-off and are comfortable with it, you're ready to begin using this method, which you do by following the steps I provide in the paragraphs that follow.

The slow way to write checks

You can write checks either from the register or from the Write Checks window. Using the Write Checks window is the slow way, but it enables you to record your expenses and the items (if any) that you purchase. Using the Write Checks window is the best choice in the following situations:

✔ You're paying for an inventory item.

✔ You're paying for something for which you have a purchase order.

✔ You plan to be reimbursed for the bill that you're paying.

✔ You want to record what job or class the bill falls under.

To use the Write Checks window to write checks, follow these steps:

1. Choose Banking➪Write Checks.

Alternatively, click the Write Checks icon in the Banking section of the Home screen. The Write Checks window appears, as shown in Figure 5-1. Notice that this window has three parts:

- *The check part on the top,* which you no doubt recognize from having written thousands of checks in the past.

- *The buttons* on the top and bottom.

- *The Expenses and Items tabs* near the middle of the window. This part is for recording what the check is for, as I explain in Steps 7, 8, and 9.

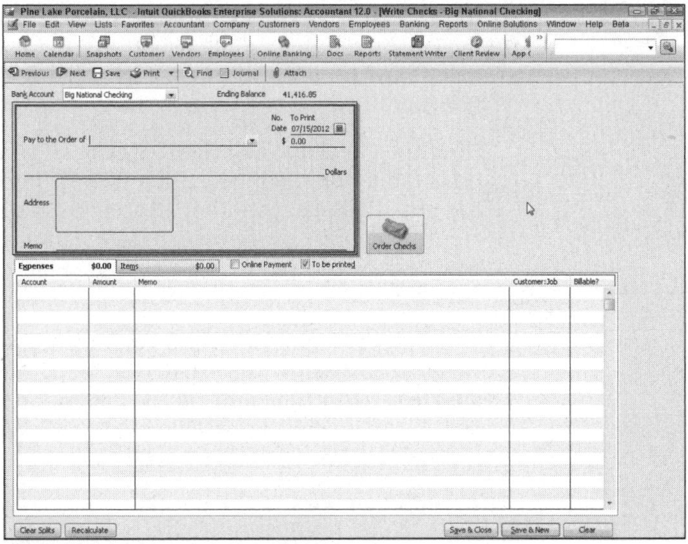

Figure 5-1: The Write Checks window.

2. Click the Bank Account drop-down list and choose the account from which you want to write this check.

This step is very important if you have more than one account. Make sure that you choose the correct account; otherwise, your account balances in QuickBooks will be incorrect.

3. Specify the check date.

Click in the Date field and type the check date. Remember that you can enter today's date by pressing the T key. You can also click the button to the right of the Date box to get a pop-up calendar. To select a date from the pop-up calendar, click the calendar day that you want to use.

4. Fill in the Pay to the Order Of line.

If you've written a check to this person or party before, the AutoFill feature fills in the name of the payee in the Pay to the Order Of line for you after you start typing the name. (AutoFill does so by comparing what you type with names shown in the Customer, Vendor, Employee, and Other Names lists.) AutoFill also puts the payee's address in the Address text box.

The AutoRecall feature can even fill out the entire check for you, based on the last check that you wrote to this vendor. (You can enable AutoRecall by choosing Edit⇨Preferences, clicking the General icon, and using the Automatically Recall Information box and buttons.)

Does the check look all right? Maybe all you need to do is tab around, adjusting numbers. Otherwise, read the next 12 steps. (Another 12-step program?) In these steps, I explain how to record information about a new vendor and pay a check to that vendor in one fell swoop.

If you've never paid anything to this person before, the program displays a Name Not Found message box after you enter the name on the Pay to the Order Of line. You can click either Quick Add or Set Up to add the payee name to one of your lists.

5. Type the amount of the check.

Now comes my favorite part. I've always found it a big bother to write out the amount of checks. I mean,

if you write a check for $21,457.00, how do you fit
"twenty-one thousand, four hundred fifty-seven dollars, and no cents" on the line? Where do you put
those hyphens, anyway?

All you have to do with QuickBooks is enter the
amount next to the dollar sign and press Tab. When
you press Tab, QuickBooks writes the amount for you
on the Dollars line. At moments like this, I'm grateful
to be alive in the 21st century, when computer technology can do these marvelous things for me.

6. (Optional) Fill in the Address text box.

You need to fill in this field only if the address isn't
there already and if you intend to send the check by
mail in a window envelope.

7. (Optional) Fill in the Memo line.

You can put a message to the payee on the Memo
line — a message, such as *Quit bleeding me dry*. But
you usually put an account number on the Memo line
so that the payee can record your account number.

If you try to click the Save & New button and close the
dialog box now, QuickBooks tells you that you can't
and tries to bite your leg off. Why? Because you can't
write a check unless you fill out the Expenses and
Items tabs. You use these tabs to describe what the
check pays.

**8. Move the cursor down to the Account column of the
Expenses tab and then enter an expense account
name.**

Chances are that you want to enter the name of an
account that's already on the Chart of Accounts.
If that's the case, move the cursor to a field in the
Account column; QuickBooks turns the field into a
drop-down list. Click the down arrow to see a list of
all your accounts. You'll probably have to scroll down
the list to get to the expense accounts. Click the one
that this check applies to — perhaps it's Rent. If you
need to create a new expense account category for
this check, choose Add New from the top of the list to
see the New Account dialog box. Fill in the information
and then click OK.

What if the money that you're paying with this check can be distributed across two, three, or four expense accounts? Simply click below the account that you just entered. The down arrow shoots down next to the cursor. Click the down arrow and enter another expense account, and another, and another, if you need to.

9. **Tab over to the Amount column, if necessary, and change around the numbers.**

    If you're distributing this check across more than one account, make sure that the numbers in the Amount column correctly distribute the check to the appropriate accounts. Figure 5-2 shows a completed check.

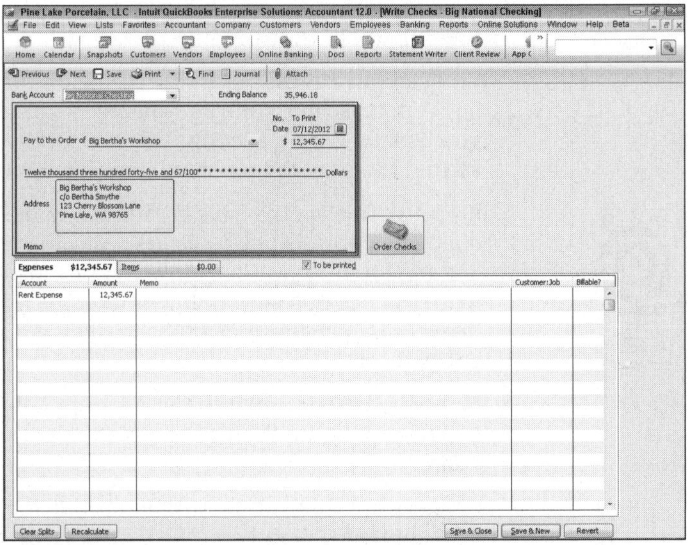

Figure 5-2: A completed check.

10. **(Optional) Enter words of explanation or encouragement in the Memo column.**

    Someday, you may have to go back to this check and try to figure out what these expenses mean. The Memo column may be your only clue. Enter some wise words here such as *August rent, copier repair,* or *company party.*

11. **(Optional) Assign the expense to the Customer:Job column.**

    If you plan to be reimbursed for these expenses, or if you just want to track your expenses by job, enter the name of the customer who is going to reimburse you. Click the down arrow to find the customer. Enter an amount for each customer or job, if necessary.

12. **(Optional) Assign the expense to a class.**

    You also can track expenses by class by making entries in the Class column. Notice the usual down arrow, which you click to see a list of classes. You won't see the Class column, however, unless you told QuickBooks that you wanted to use classes when you created your company. (You create the company when you work your way through the QuickBooks Setup; see Chapter 1.)

     If you want to have QuickBooks track expenses by class, you have to set it up to do so. To set up QuickBooks to track expenses, choose Edit⇨Preferences. When QuickBooks displays the Preferences dialog box, click the Accounting icon, click the Company Preferences tab, and then check the Use Class Tracking check box.

13. **Use the Items tab to record what you're purchasing.**

    You may be purchasing inventory items, or you may already have filled out a purchase order for the items for which you're paying. If either of these cases is so, click the Items tab. If you don't have a purchase order for the items, go on to Step 14. If you do have a purchase order for the items, click the Select PO button to see a list of purchases on order with this vendor. Check those for which you're paying, and click OK.

     QuickBooks doesn't show its purchase order (PO) feature unless you told it during the QuickBooks Setup that you want to use purchase orders. If you now think you want to use them, choose Edit⇨Preferences. When QuickBooks displays the Preferences dialog box, click the Items & Inventory button, click the Company Preferences tab, and then select the Inventory and Purchase Orders Are Active check box.

14. Move the cursor to the Item column and enter a name for the item.

Notice the down arrow in this column. Click the arrow to see the Items list. Does the item that you're paying for appear on this list? If so, click it. If not, choose Add New from the top of the list and fill out the New Item window. (Read about this in Chapter 2.)

15. Fill in the rest of the rows of items on the Items tab.

You can enter all the items that you're purchasing on this tab. Make sure that the Items tab accurately shows the items that you're purchasing, their cost, and the quantity.

When you finish adding items, you may want to use one of the following options that appear in the Write Checks window:

- Click the *Print button* to print the check in the Write Checks window. This option doesn't print all the checks that you have written and marked to be printed, however.

- The *Clear Splits button* deletes any individual amounts that you entered for separate expenses or items on the Expenses and Items tabs. Then QuickBooks enters the total amount of the check in the Amount column on the Expenses tab.

- The *Recalculate button* totals the items and expenses in the window. It also puts the total on both the numeric and text amount lines of the check.

- The *To Be Printed check box* designates the check for printing. Select this check box if you want to print the check with QuickBooks by using your printer and preprinted check forms. Clear this check box if you're recording a hand-written check.

- The *Online Payment check box* (if you've enabled online bill pay) lets you specify that you want to specify that the particular check you're describing is an "online payment."

16. Click the Save & New button or the Save & Close button to finish writing the check.

Click Save & Close to tell QuickBooks that you want to save the check and close the check form. Click Save & New to tell QuickBooks that you want to save the check and then display another blank check form. If you don't want to save the check, close the dialog box and then click No when QuickBooks asks whether you want to save the check.

You can also use the Next and Previous buttons to move to previously written checks or to a blank check form. If you write check number 101, for example, clicking Next takes you to check 102 so that you can write that one. (Clicking Previous moves you to check 100, in case you need to edit a check that you've written earlier.)

Well, that's over with. For a minute there, I thought that it would never end.

The fast way to write checks

If you want to pay a bill that isn't for inventory, that you won't be reimbursed for, or that you don't need to track in any way, shape, or form, you can write your check directly from the Checking register. This method is the fast and easy way to go. Follow these steps:

1. **Choose Banking⇨Use Register.**

   Alternatively, click the Register icon in the Banking section on the Home page. The register appears, as shown in Figure 5-3. (If you have more than one bank account, you have to choose the proper account from the drop-down list and click OK.) The cursor is at the end of the register, ready and waiting for you to enter check information.

2. **Fill in the information for the check.**

   Notice that the entries you make are the same ones that you'd make on a check. You need to note three things about the register:

   • If you enter a Payee name that QuickBooks doesn't recognize, you see the Name Not Found message box, and you're asked to give information about this new, mysterious vendor. To see what to do next, read the preceding set of instructions on writing a check the slow way.

- You have to choose an account name. Chances are good that you can find the right one in the Account drop-down list; if you can't, though, enter one of your own. QuickBooks displays the Account Not Found message box and asks you to fill in the information about this new account.

- To record a check that pays more than a single expense, click the Splits button (in the bottom-left corner of the window) to display a little box that you can use to input multiple expense accounts and amounts.

As you fill out the register, if you decide that you want to be reimbursed for this check or that you want to track expenses and items, click the Edit Transaction button. You see the Write Checks window; refer to Figure 5-1. Follow Steps 3–14 in the preceding section on how to write a check the slow way to fill in the Write Checks window. When you finish filling in the Write Checks window, click Save & New. You're back where you started, in the register window.

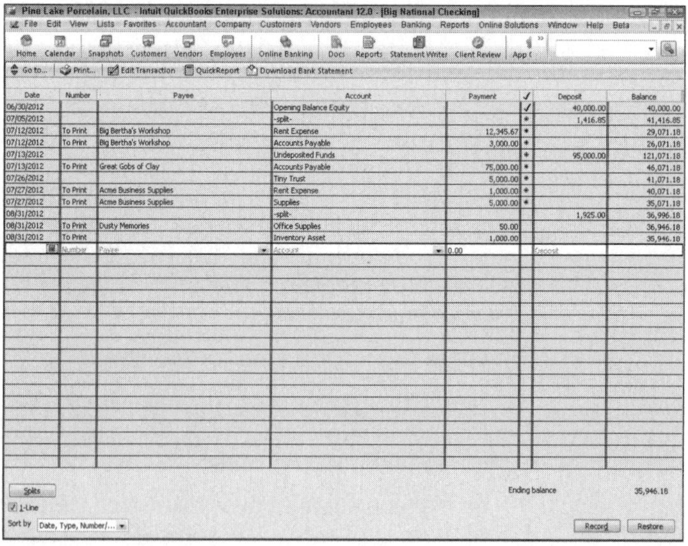

Figure 5-3: The register.

3. **When you finish filling in the check information, click the Record button.**

   You click Record, of course, to record the check.

   By the way, if you realize that you made a mistake and haven't yet clicked Record to record the check, you can click the Restore button to go back to square one. Clicking Restore blanks out what you just entered so that you can start over again.

Recording Your Bills the Accounts Payable Way

The accounts payable (A/P) way of paying bills involves two steps. The first is a trifle on the difficult side, and the second step is as easy as pie. First, you record your bills. If you read the section earlier in this chapter on writing checks the slow way, you're already familiar with using the Expenses tab and the Items tab to record bills. You need to fill out those tabs for the A/P method as well if you want to distribute a bill to accounts, customers, jobs, classes, and items. If you read the first half of this chapter, some of what follows will be old hat.

After you record your bills, you can go on to the second step: telling QuickBooks which bills to pay. Then QuickBooks writes the checks. You print them. You mail them.

To make the A/P method work, you have to record your bills as they come in. That doesn't mean that you have to pay them right away. By recording your bills, you can keep track of how much money you owe and how much money your business really has. QuickBooks reminds you when your bills are due so that you don't have to worry about forgetting to pay a bill.

When you record bills the accounts payable way, you're using accrual-basis accounting.

Recording your bills

When a bill comes in, the first thing to do is record it. You can record bills through the Enter Bills window or the Accounts Payable register. If you plan to track bills by expense and item, you need to use the Enter Bills window. I describe that method first. If you have a simple bill to pay that doesn't need to be reimbursed or tracked, skip ahead to the "Paying Your Bills" section, later in this chapter.

To record a bill through the Enter Bills window, follow these steps:

1. **Choose Vendors⇨Enter Bills.**

   Alternatively, click the Enter Bills icon in the Vendors area on the Home page. Figure 5-4 shows the Enter Bills window. You no doubt notice that the top half of this window looks a great deal like a check, and that's because much of the information that you put here ends up on the check that you write to pay your bill. (If you see the word *Credit* at the top of the form rather than *Bill,* select the Bill radio button in the top-left corner. You also can use this screen to enter credit memos from vendors.)

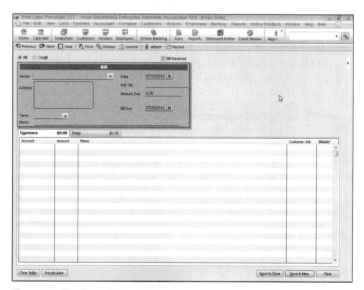

Figure 5-4: The Enter Bills window.

2. **Select the name of the vendor whom you're paying.**

   If you want to pay this bill to a vendor who's already on the Vendor list, click the down arrow at the end of the Vendor line and choose the vendor. (Then QuickBooks automatically fills the Enter Bills window with as much information as it can remember.) If this vendor is new, QuickBooks asks you to Quick Add or Set Up some information about the vendor: the address, credit limit, payment terms, and so on. You provide this information in the New Vendor window. If you aren't familiar with this window, make a brief visit to Chapter 2.

If you have one or more unfilled purchase orders with the vendor that you select, QuickBooks asks you whether you want to receive against a purchase order. Click Yes if you do or No if you don't. If you choose to receive against a purchase order, QuickBooks displays the Open Purchase Orders dialog box, as shown in Figure 5-5. It lists the open purchase orders you've recorded. When you select one or more purchase orders to receive against, QuickBooks fills in the items and amounts from these orders for you, which you can modify as necessary. When you finish with the Purchase Orders dialog box, click OK to get back to the Enter Bills window.

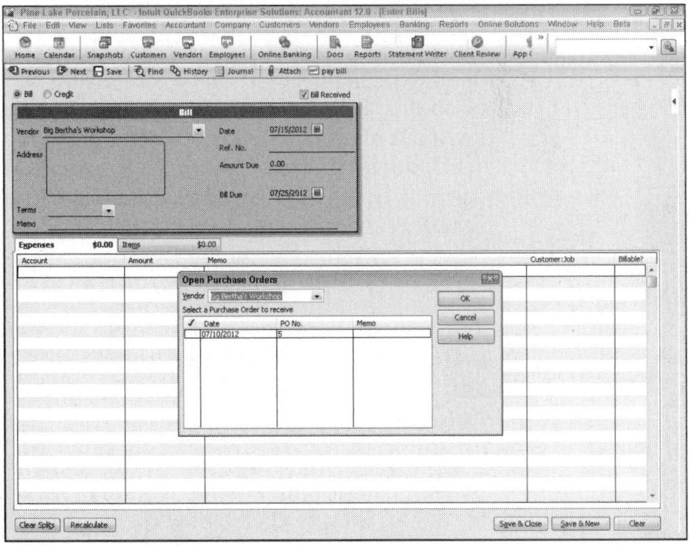

Figure 5-5: Paying a bill against a purchase order.

To create a *purchase order,* which is a record of items you order from vendors, choose Vendors⇨Create Purchase Orders. When QuickBooks displays the Create Purchase Orders window, describe your order. You print and edit purchase orders, by the way, in the same manner as you print invoices and credit memos.

3. **Select the payment terms that describe when the bill is due.**

   On the Terms line, open the drop-down list and choose the payment terms (if the information isn't already there from when you set up the vendor).

4. **(Optional) Enter the vendor's reference number.**

   If you enter the vendor's reference number for the bill — this is probably just the invoice number or your account number — the reference number prints on the voucher that's part of the printed check.

5. **(Optional) Enter a memo to describe the bill.**

   You can enter a note in the Memo text box. The note that you enter appears on the A/P register.

6. **Move the cursor down to the Account column of the Expenses tab and enter an expense account name.**

   Chances are good that you want to enter the name of an expense account that's already on the Chart of Accounts. If that's the case, click the down arrow to see a list of all your accounts. You probably have to scroll down the list to get to the expense accounts. (A fast way to move down the list is to start typing the account name; you go straight down the list.) Click the account that this bill represents. (Most likely, it's Supplies or something like that.)

   If you need to create a new expense account category for this bill, choose Add New from the top of the list. You see the New Account dialog box. Fill in the information, and click OK.

   What if the money that you're paying out because of this bill can be split among two, three, or four expense accounts? Simply click below the account that you just entered. The down arrow appears. Click it to enter another expense account, and another, and another, if you need to.

7. **Tab over to the Amount column, if necessary, and change the numbers.**

   If you're splitting this bill among several accounts, make sure that the numbers in the Amount column add to the total of the bill.

8. **(Optional) Enter words of explanation or wisdom in the Memo column.**

9. **(Optional) Assign the expense to a Customer:Job.**

   If you plan to be reimbursed for these expenses, or if you just want to track your expenses by job, enter the customer who is going to reimburse you. Enter an amount for each account if necessary. You can use the down arrow to find customers and then click them.

10. **(Optional) Assign the expense to a class.**

    You also can track expenses by class by making entries in the Class column. Notice the usual down arrow, and click it to see a list of classes. (You don't see a Class column unless you told QuickBooks that you want to use classes.)

    If you want to have QuickBooks track expenses by class, you can set it up to do so. To set up QuickBooks to track expenses, choose Edit⇨Preferences. When QuickBooks displays the Preferences dialog box, click the Accounting icon, click the Company Preferences tab, and then select the Use Class Tracking check box.

    If you want, click the Recalculate button to total the expenses.

11. **Use the Items tab to record the various items that the bill represents.**

    Click the Items tab. Enter the items you purchased and the prices you paid for them.

    If you realize after partially completing the bill that the bill does indeed pay a purchase order, click the Select PO button, which appears on the Items tab of the Enter Bills window.

    From the Vendor drop-down list, choose the name of the vendor who sent you the bill. In the list of open purchase orders, click in the column on the left to put a check mark next to the purchase order (or orders) for which you're paying. Easy enough? Click OK when you're done; QuickBooks fills out the Items tab for you automatically.

12. **Move to the Item column and enter a name for the item.**

    Notice the down arrow in this column. Click it to see the Item list. Does the item that you're paying for appear on this list? If so, click that item. If not, choose Add New from the top of the list and fill out the New Item window. (See Chapter 2.)

13. **Fill in the rest of the rows of items on the Items tab.**

    You can enter all the items you're purchasing here. Make sure that the Items tab accurately shows the items that you're purchasing, their costs, and their quantities. If you want to, click the Recalculate button to total the items.

14. **Save the bill.**

    Click Save & New to save your record of the bill and then enter another bill. Or click Save & Close to record your bill but not enter another bill.

Just as in the case with customer-related windows (like the Create Invoices window), QuickBooks lets you add and remove historical information about a vendor from and to the Enter Bills window and many other "vendor information" windows. To add historical vendor information to a window, click the Show History button that appears in the upper-right corner of the window. You click links in the Show History panel to drill down and get even more information about, for example, a listed transaction.

Entering your bills the fast way

You also can enter bills directly in the Accounts Payable register. This method is faster, but it makes tracking expenses and items more difficult.

If you want to enter bills directly in the Accounts Payable register, follow these steps:

1. **Choose Lists⇨Chart of Accounts or click the Chart of Accounts icon on the Home page.**

   The Chart of Accounts opens.

2. **Open the Accounts Payable account.**

   When QuickBooks displays your Chart of Accounts, double-click the Accounts Payable account in the list. You see the Accounts Payable register window, as shown in Figure 5-6. The cursor is at the end of the register, ready and waiting for you to enter the next bill.

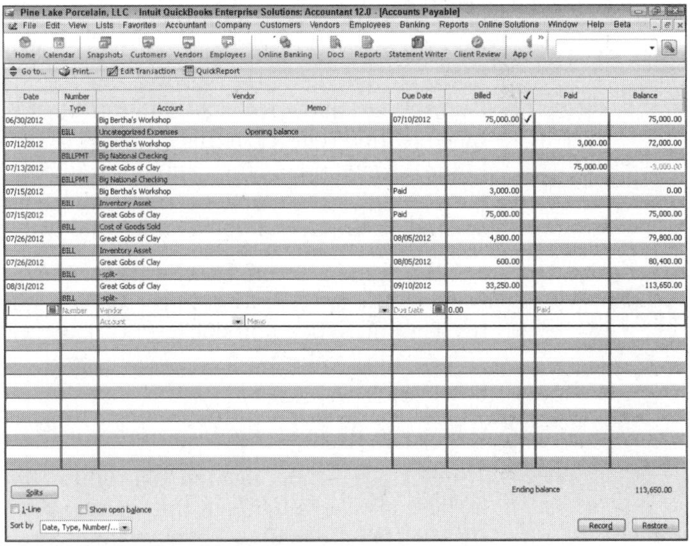

Figure 5-6: The Accounts Payable register window.

3. **Fill in the information for your bill.**

   Enter the same information that you would if you were filling in the Enter Bills window that I describe at the beginning of this chapter. In the Vendor text box, click the down arrow and choose a name from the Vendor list.

   If you enter a vendor name that QuickBooks doesn't recognize, you see the Vendor Not Found message box, and QuickBooks asks you to give information about this new, mysterious vendor. Either click Quick Add to have the program collect the information from the register as you fill it out or click Set Up to see the New Vendor dialog box. (I explain how to set up new vendors in Chapter 2.)

You have to select an account name. You can probably find the right one in the Account drop-down list; if you can't, enter one of your own. You see the Account Not Found message box, and QuickBooks asks you to fill in information about this new account.

If you decide while you fill out the register that you want to be reimbursed for this check or that you want to track expenses and items, click the Edit Transaction button to see the Enter Bills window (as shown in Figure 5-4). Follow Steps 2–12 in the "Recording your bills" section (earlier in this chapter) to fill in the Enter Bills window. When you finish filling in the window, click Save & New. You're back where you started: in the Accounts Payable window.

See the Splits button? This Splits button works the same as the Splits button in the bank account register window. When you click Splits, QuickBooks provides additional rows for inputting expense and class information.

4. When you fill in all the information, click Record.

The Restore button, located just right of Record, is there in case you fill out the register but decide that you want to start all over again before you've recorded the transaction. Click Restore to clear the information onscreen, and you have a clean slate.

Deleting a bill

Suppose that you accidentally enter the same bill twice or enter a bill that was really meant for the business next door. (Just because you're tracking bills by computer doesn't mean that you don't have to look over things carefully anymore.) Here's how to delete a bill that you entered in the Accounts Payable register:

1. **Locate the bill in the Accounts Payable register by using one of the following methods:**

    • *If you know roughly what day you entered the bill,* you can scroll through the list to find it. The entries are listed in date order. (Select the 1-Line check box to display each bill on one line rather than on two lines to make the scrolling go faster.)

    • *If you don't remember the date,* use the Edit menu's Find command.

    And now, back to the Accounts Payable register window that you have in progress. . . .

2. **Select the bill that you want to delete by clicking anywhere in the bill.**

3. **Choose Edit⇨Delete Bill.**

    QuickBooks confirms that you really, truly want to delete the transaction. If you click OK, it dutifully deletes the bill from the A/P register.

Remind me to pay that bill, will you?

You could tie a string around your finger, but the best way to make sure that you pay your bills on time is to have QuickBooks remind you. In fact, you can make the Reminders message box the first thing that you see when you start QuickBooks.

To adjust the QuickBooks reminder options, you must be logged on as the administrator in single-user mode. Then choose Edit⇨Preferences. When QuickBooks displays the Preferences dialog box, click the Reminders icon from the list on the left and then click the Company Preferences tab to access the dialog box shown in Figure 5-7, with the Reminders item on the list.

Make sure that its Show Summary or Show List option button is selected and then give yourself several days' notice before you need to pay bills by typing a number (10 is the default and usually works well) in the Days Before Due Date text box, in the Remind Me column.

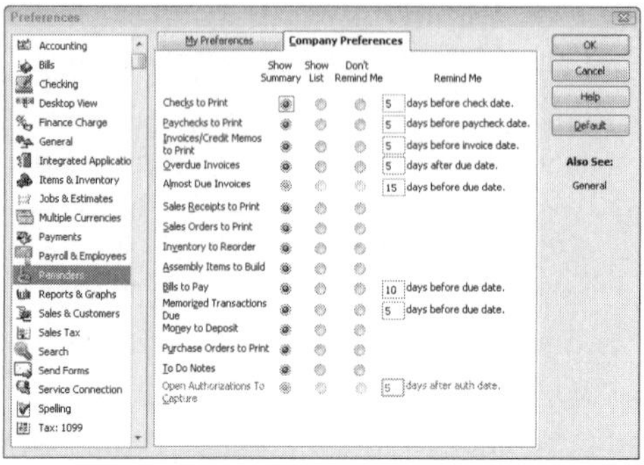

Figure 5-7: The Preferences dialog box.

If you select the Show Summary option (the first button to the right of the option), you get a summary of the bills that you owe each time you start QuickBooks. If you select Show List (the second button to the right of the option), you get the details about each bill.

Be sure to review the Reminders window when you start QuickBooks or open a new company file. The window lists reminders (such as forms you need to print and payments you need to transmit) and tells you which unpaid bills you're supposed to pay. You can see this list by choosing Company⇨Reminders.

Paying Your Bills

If you've done everything right and recorded your bills correctly, writing checks is a snap. Just follow these steps:

1. **Choose Vendors⇨Pay Bills.**

   Alternatively, click the Pay Bills icon located on the Home page. You see the Pay Bills window, as shown in Figure 5-8.

2. **Change the Payment Date (at the bottom) to the date that you want to appear on the checks.**

   By default, this field shows today's date. If you want another date on the payment check — for example, if you're postdating the check — change this date.

(See the online Cheat Sheet at www.dummies.com/
cheatsheet/quickbooks2012 for some secret date-
editing codes.)

3. **Set a cutoff date for showing bills.**

   In the Show Bills Due On or Before date field, tell
   QuickBooks which bills to show by entering a date. If
   you want to see all the bills, select the Show All Bills
   radio button.

4. **Use the Sort By drop-down list to tell QuickBooks
   how to sort the bills.**

   You can arrange bills by due date with the oldest bills
   listed first, arrange them alphabetically by vendor, or
   arrange them from largest to smallest.

5. **Identify which bills to pay.**

   If you want to pay all the bills in the dialog box, click the
   Select All Bills button. If you want to clear all the bills you
   marked, click the Clear Selections button. If you want
   to pick and choose, click to the left of the bill's due date
   to pay the bill. A check mark appears where you click.
   Note that after you apply a payment, the Clear Selections
   button replaces the Select All Bills button.

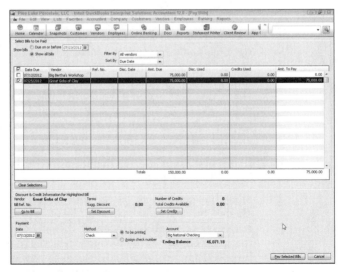

Figure 5-8: The Pay Bills window.

6. Change the Amt. to Pay figure if you want to pay only part of a bill.

That's right — you can pay only part of a bill by changing the number in the Amt. to Pay column. (Of course, they can always just send you another bill. . . .)

7. Get the early payment discount rate on your bills, if any.

You may be eligible for an early payment discount on some bills. To find out how much of a discount you get, click the Amt. to Pay field and then click the Set Discount button to see the Discount tab of the Discount and Credits dialog box. Use the Discount tab's Amount of Discount box to give the dollar amount of the discount. Use the Discount tab's Discount Account box to specify which account should be used for recording the money saved through the discount.

8. Get a list of credit memos that you can apply to the payment.

Click the Set Credits button to see the Credits tab of the Discount and Credits dialog box. If you want to use one of the credits listed to reduce the amount of the bill, click it and then click Done.

9. Select a payment date, method, and bank account.

Use the Payment area's Date field to specify when the bill should be paid, the Method drop-down list to select the payment method you want to use (Check or Credit Card), and the Account drop-down list to select the bank account from which payment will be made. (*Note:* If you've subscribed to and set up the QuickBooks online bill payment feature, you have another payment method choice: online payment.)

10. If you plan to print the check, select the To Be Printed option button.

Many businesses use QuickBooks to keep track of checks, but instead of printing the checks, they have employees write them by hand. If your business uses this method, select the Assign Check Number radio button. Then, when QuickBooks asks how it should number the check, either give the number by typing

it into the appropriate box or tell QuickBooks to automatically number the check.

11. **Click the Pay Selected Bills button to pay the bills
and close the Pay Bills window.**

QuickBooks goes into the Accounts Payable register
and notes that you paid these bills; then it goes into the
register and "writes" the check or checks. Figures 5-9
and 5-10 show you exactly what I mean. (The two figures show a $75,000 bill from Great Gobs of Clay being
paid.)

Date	Number	Payee	Account	Payment	✓	Deposit	Balance
06/30/2012			Opening Balance Equity		✓	40,000.00	40,000.00
07/05/2012			-split-		*	1,416.85	41,416.85
07/12/2012	To Print	Big Bertha's Workshop	Rent Expense	12,345.67	*		29,071.18
07/12/2012	To Print	Big Bertha's Workshop	Accounts Payable	3,000.00	*		26,071.18
07/13/2012			Undeposited Funds		*	95,000.00	121,071.18
07/13/2012	To Print	Great Gobs of Clay	Accounts Payable	75,000.00	*		46,071.18
07/26/2012			Tiny Trust	5,000.00	*		41,071.18
07/27/2012	To Print	Acme Business Supplies	Rent Expense	1,000.00	*		40,071.18
07/27/2012	To Print	Acme Business Supplies	Supplies	5,000.00	*		35,071.18
08/31/2012			-split-			1,925.00	36,996.18
08/31/2012	To Print	Dusty Memories	Office Supplies	50.00			36,946.18
08/31/2012	To Print		Inventory Asset	1,000.00			35,946.18

Ending balance   35,946.18

Figure 5-9: How a paid bill looks in the register. Oooh. Cool.

QuickBooks shows the original bill amount as the amount
that's paid, not the original bill amount minus the early payment discount. It needs to use this method to completely pay
off the bill.

In the Accounts Payable register, you see BILLPMT in the
Type column and the amount paid in the Paid column. The
Due Date and Billed columns are now empty.

In the register, you again see BILLPMT in the Type column.

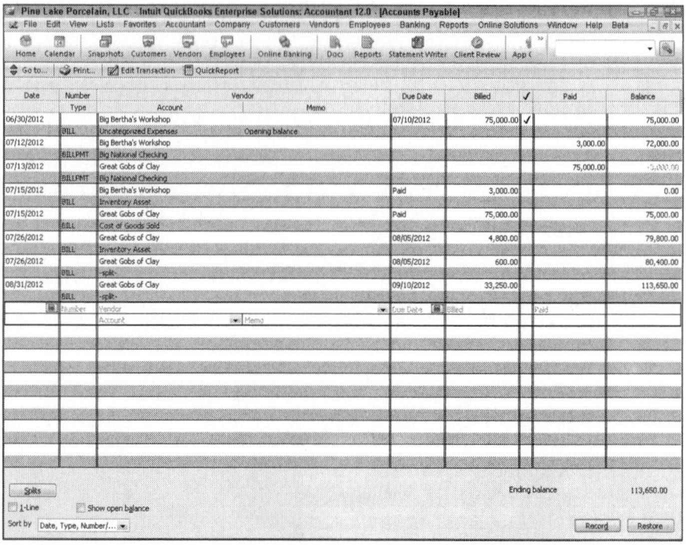

Figure 5-10: How the check that pays a bill looks in the Accounts Payable register.

But don't kid yourself — these bills aren't really paid yet. Sure, they're paid in the mind of QuickBooks, but the mind of QuickBooks extends only as far as the metal (or trendy plastic) box that holds your computer. You still have to write or print the checks and deliver them to the payees.

If you're going to write the checks by hand, enter the check numbers from your own checkbook into the QuickBooks register Number column. You want these numbers to jibe, not jive. (I know: A pun is the lowest form of humor.)

And another thing: If you enter a bill, you absolutely must use the Pay Bills command to record the payment that pays off the bill. If you don't do this, the unpaid bill just sits there forever, lonely and forlorn.

Tracking Vehicle Mileage

QuickBooks includes a vehicle mileage-tracking feature that lets you track your business miles. To track vehicle mileage in QuickBooks, choose Company⇨Enter Vehicle Mileage. Then, in the Enter Vehicle Mileage dialog box that appears, record the vehicle, date, miles driven, odometer settings, and reason for the trip.

May I briefly tell you the IRS rules for deducting business miles? Essentially, you have two approaches to choose between. The easier method — and the one that I use, because I'm lazy — is to record as a business expense an amount per business mile driven. The rate per mile is roughly $0.55, which is far less than the actual cost of driving most cars. But, hey — that's the price of slothfulness.

The hard method for tracking business miles is to track all your vehicle expenses — including gas, oil, repairs, insurance, and vehicle depreciation — and then record as a business expense the business-use portion of these expenses.

To get the business-use portion of your vehicle, use the ratio of business miles to total miles. For example, if during the year, you drive 6,000 business miles and your total miles are 12,000, your business-use percentage equals 50 percent. In this case, you can record as a business expense 50 percent of your vehicle expenses.

Usually with the hard "actual expenses" method, you get a higher business vehicle expense deduction. However, you should note that the IRS limits the amount that you can include as vehicle depreciation, so you don't get as high a deduction as you might at first think. (You may want to consult your tax advisor for details.)

No matter which method you use, you want a record of your actual business miles, which the Enter Vehicle Mileage command enables you to do. By law, you need a good record of business mileage to legitimately claim the deduction.

Paying Sales Tax

To ingratiate itself with you retailers, QuickBooks includes a special dialog box for paying sales tax. However, to use this dialog box, you must have sales tax items or a sales tax group already set up. See Chapter 2 for a thorough explanation of items and groups.

To see how much sales tax you owe and to write checks to government agencies in one fell swoop, choose Vendors⇨ Sales Tax⇨Pay Sales Tax to access the Pay Sales Tax dialog box, as shown in Figure 5-11. Alternatively, click the Pay Sales Tax icon on the Home page in the Vendors area.

Pay Sales Tax			
Pay From Account	Check Date	Show sales tax due through	Starting Check No.
Big National Checking	07/31/2012	07/31/2012	To Print
P... Item	Vendor	Amt. Due	Amt. Paid
WSST			
		Totals	12.50	0.00
Pay All Tax	Adjust	Ending Bank Balance	46,071.18
☑ To be printed		OK	Cancel	Help

Figure 5-11: The Pay Sales Tax dialog box.

This dialog box is similar to the Pay Bills window (refer to Figure 5-8). The buttons basically work the same way.

Click in the Pay column to add check marks next to all the items that you want to pay. QuickBooks automatically writes checks in the Checking register. Your payments are likewise recorded in the Sales Tax Payable register.

If the state or local tax agency in your area allows a discount for timely sales tax remittals, you should know about the Vendors⇨Sales Tax⇨Adjust Sales Tax Due command. When you choose this command, QuickBooks displays the Sales Tax Adjustment dialog box, which lets you adjust the sales tax liability you owe some government agency for something like a discount.

Chapter 6

Reporting on the State of Affairs

● ●

In This Chapter

▶ Printing QuickBooks reports

▶ Using the Reports menu commands

▶ QuickZooming report totals

▶ Sharing information with a spreadsheet

▶ Editing and rearranging report information

▶ Processing multiple reports

▶ Using QuickReports

● ●

*T*o find out whether your business is thriving or diving, you use the QuickBooks Reports feature. The different kinds of reports in QuickBooks cover everything from cash flow to missing checks, not to mention QuickReports. *QuickReports* are summary reports that you can get from the information on forms, account registers, or lists by merely clicking the mouse.

In this chapter, I tell you how to prepare reports, how to print them, and how to customize reports for your special needs.

What Kinds of Reports Are There, Anyway?

If you run a small business, you don't need all the reports that QuickBooks offers, but many of these reports are extremely useful. Reports show you how healthy or unhealthy your business is, where your profits are, and where you're wasting time and squandering resources.

To make sense of what might otherwise become mass confusion, QuickBooks organizes all its reports in categories. You can see all the categories by pulling down the Reports menu or by clicking the Report Center icon. The names of the reports read a bit like public television documentary names, don't they? "Tonight, Joob Taylor explores the mazelike federal budget in Budget Reports." You select a report category to see a list of report names.

In Table 6-1, I describe reports by category and give a short description of the major reports in each category. To get a thorough description of a particular report, go to the Help feature. To find out what a standard profit and loss report does, for example, choose Help➪QuickBooks Help and then click the Index tab. Type **financial statements** in the text box. (The Help information includes a wonderful discussion about how to understand the profit and loss and balance sheet financial statements.) Or, from the Reports Center, select the type of report on the left; you see a list of the different reports available on the right side, with a description of the information contained in each one. To read the details about a topic, click that topic in the list.

Table 6-1	QuickBooks Report Categories
Report Category	*Description*
Company & Financial	These reports give you a bird's-eye view of your company's health and cash flow. They give you a snapshot of your assets, liabilities, and equity, showing income, expenses, and net profit or loss over time.
Customers & Receivables	These accounts receivable reports are great for finding out where you stand in regard to your customer invoices. You can list unpaid invoices and group them in various ways, including by customer, job, and aging status.
Sales	These reports show what you sold and who your customers are. You can see your sales by item, by customer, or by sales representative.

Report Category	Description
Jobs, Time & Mileage	These reports let you see job and item profitability, compare job estimates versus actual costs, view time recorded on jobs and activities, and look at vehicle mileage.
Vendors & Payables	These accounts payable reports tell you everything you need to know about your unpaid bills. You can list bills in a variety of ways, including by vendor and by aging status. This category also includes a report for determining sales tax liability.
Purchases	If you enable the Items and Purchases option within QuickBooks when you run QuickBooks Setup, these reports show from whom you bought, what you bought, and how much you paid. You can list purchases by item or by vendor. One handy report shows any outstanding purchase orders.
Inventory	These reports help answer the ever-important question, "What items do I have in stock?" You can get an enormous amount of detail from these reports. For example, you can find out how many of an item you have on hand and how many you have on order. You can group inventory by vendor or by item. If you need price lists, you can print them by using a special report from your QuickBooks file.
Employees & Payroll	These reports, available if you signed up for one of the QuickBooks payroll options, offer ways to track payroll or check your payroll liability accounts. Believe me: These reports come in handy.
Banking	These reports list checks and deposits.
Accountant & Taxes	These reports include income tax reports, journal and general ledger reports, and a trial balance.

(continued)

Table 6-1 *(continued)*

Report Category	Description
Budgets & Forecasts	These reports show you once and for all whether your budgeting skills are realistic. You can view budgets by job, by month, or by balance sheet account. Then you can compare the budgets with actual income and expense totals. (You need to have a budget already set up to use this report.)
List	These reports let you see your lists in detail. For example, you can see the contacts, phone numbers, and addresses on your Customer, Vendor, or Other Names lists. You also can create a detailed report of your inventory.
Industry Specific	Some versions of QuickBooks also supply industry-specific reports under the Industry Specific submenu command. QuickBooks, at the time of this writing, provides industry-specific versions of QuickBooks for accountants, contractors, manufacturers, wholesalers, professional service firms, retailers, and nonprofit organizations.

If you're not sure which specific report you want, you can use the Report Center. Just choose Reports➪Report Center and choose a report category from the list along the left edge of the Report Center window (see Figure 6-1). QuickBooks displays a picture of the most common reports within the category in the Report Center window.

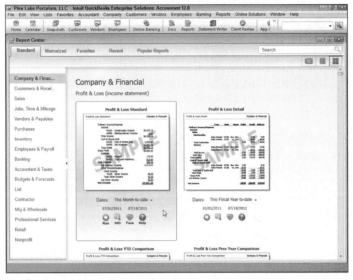

Figure 6-1: The Report Center window.

Creating and Printing a Report

After you decide what report you need, all you have to do is
select it from the appropriate menu or from the Report Center
window. To create a standard profit and loss report, for example, choose Reports⇨Company & Financial⇨Profit & Loss
Standard or select it from the Report Center. Or, double-click
the report image in the Report Center window.

Depending on how much data QuickBooks has to process,
you may see a Building Report box before the report appears
onscreen in all its glory. Figure 6-2 shows a standard profit
and loss report, or an *income statement.*

If you see a Customize Report dialog box instead of a report, you can tell QuickBooks to change this option. To do so, choose Edit⇨Preferences and then click the Reports & Graphs icon in the list on the left. Click the My Preferences tab, if you have one and it isn't already selected. Remove the check mark from the Prompt Me to Modify Report Options Before Opening a Report check box.

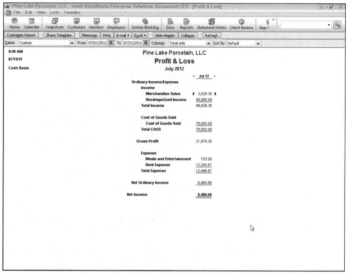

Figure 6-2: A standard profit and loss report.

You can't see the entire onscreen version of a report unless your report is very small (or your screen is monstrously large). Use the Page Up and Page Down keys on your keyboard to scroll up and down, and use the Tab and Shift+Tab keys to move left and right. Or, if you're a mouse lover, you can use the scroll bar.

To print a report, click the Print button at the top of the report. QuickBooks displays the Print Reports dialog box, as shown in Figure 6-3. To accept the given specifications, which are almost always fine, click the Print button. You'll never guess what happens next: QuickBooks prints the report!

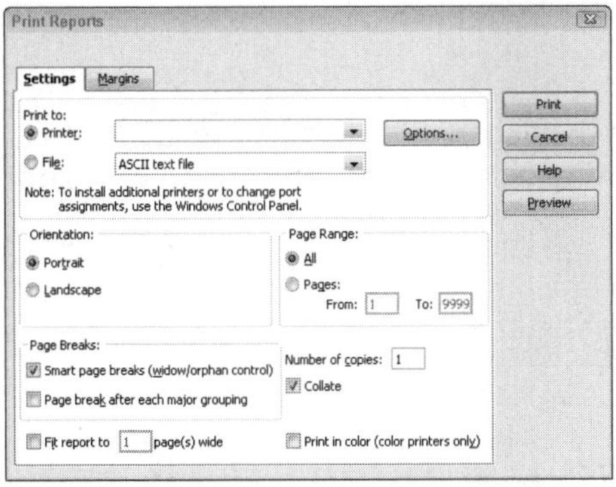

Figure 6-3: The Print Reports dialog box.

The first time you print a report, QuickBooks displays a Printing Features dialog box that explains a few things about the mechanics of choosing and printing reports.

Before I forget, I want to tell you that you can select the File radio button in the Print To panel to tell QuickBooks to save the report as a file instead of printing it. You can then choose the file format: ASCII Text File, Comma Delimited File, or Tab Delimited File. You can use either delimited-file format if you want to open the file later with a spreadsheet program, such as Microsoft Excel. After you click Print, use the Create Disk File dialog box to specify the filename and storage location.

The File menu includes a Save as PDF command, which you can use to create a PDF version of the report that shows in the report menu. Just choose the command and provide a name for the PDF when QuickBooks prompts.

The Orientation settings tell QuickBooks how the report is supposed to appear on the paper. The Page Range settings specify the pages that you want to print. The Fit Report to *xx* Page(s) Wide check box enables you to shrink the report so that it fits on the number of pages you specify. The purpose of the Print in Color (Color Printers Only) check box is pretty self-evident.

QuickBooks includes two page-break options for creating easier-to-read reports:

- Select the first check box (Smart page breaks) to keep items that belong in the same group on the same page.
- Select the second check box to give each major group its own page.

You also can preview the report by clicking the Preview button.

Visiting the report dog-and-pony show

You can do some neat things with the reports you create. Here's a quick rundown of some of the most valuable tricks:

- **QuickZooming mysterious figures:** If you don't understand where a number in a report comes from, point to it with the mouse. As you point to numbers, QuickBooks changes the mouse pointer to a magnifying glass marked with a *Z.* Double-click the mouse to have QuickBooks display a list of all the transactions that make up that number.

  This feature, called *QuickZoom,* is extremely handy for understanding the figures that appear on reports. All you have to do is double-click any mysterious-looking figure in a report. QuickBooks immediately tells you exactly how it arrived at that figure.

- **Sharing report data with Microsoft Excel:** You can export report data to an Excel spreadsheet by clicking the Excel button in the report window. When QuickBooks displays its menu, choose either the Create New Worksheet or Update Existing Worksheet command. (QuickBooks will display the Send Report to Excel dialog box, which you can use to exercise additional control over how the report gets sent to Microsoft Excel.)

Editing and rearranging reports

You may have noticed that when QuickBooks displays the report document window, it also displays a row of buttons:

Modify Report, Memorize, Print, E-Mail, Export, and so on (refer to Figure 6-2). Below this toolbar are some drop-down lists that have to do with dates, a drop-down list called Columns, and a drop-down list called Sort By. (Not all these lists are available in every report document window. I don't know why, really. Maybe just to keep you guessing.)

You don't need to worry about these buttons and lists. Read through the discussion that follows only if you're feeling comfortable, relaxed, and truly mellow, okay?

Modifying

When you click the Customize Report button, QuickBooks displays the Modify Report dialog box, as shown in Figure 6-4. From this dialog box, you can change the information displayed on a report and the way that information is arranged (by using the Display tab); the data used to generate the report (by using the Filters tab); the header and footer information (by using, predictably, the Header/Footer tab); and the typeface and size of print used for a report (by using the Fonts & Numbers tab).

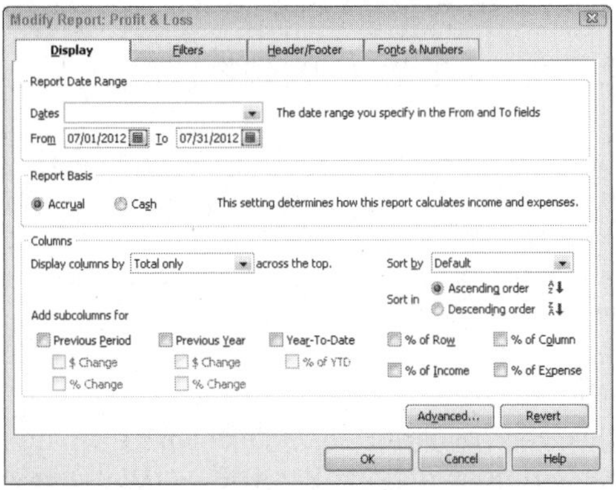

Figure 6-4: The Modify Report dialog box.

Sharing templates

If you work in a multiple-user QuickBooks environment and you create a customized report, you can share this report with other users. To do this, click the Share Template button. When QuickBooks displays the Share Template dialog box (not shown), name and describe the shared report using the

Report Title and Description text boxes. Then click the Share button.

Memorizing

If you do play around with the remaining buttons, you can save any custom report specifications that you create. Just click the Memorize button. QuickBooks displays the Memorize Report dialog box (shown in Figure 6-5), which asks you to supply a name for the customized report and assign the memorized report to a report group. After you name and assign the customized report, QuickBooks lists it whenever you choose Reports⇨Memorized Reports and then click the report group. You can also access Memorized Reports from the top of the Report Center screen. Whenever you want to use your special report, all you need to do is choose it from the list and click the Report button.

Memorize Report		
Name:	Profit & Loss	
☐ Save in Memorized Report Group:	Accountant	▼
☐ Share this report template with others		
OK	Cancel	

Figure 6-5: The Memorize Report dialog box.

QuickBooks memorizes the print orientation with the report, so if the print orientation isn't the way you want it for the report, you should first change it by choosing File⇨Printer Setup. Select the orientation you want to memorize, click OK, and then memorize the report.

E-mailing

If you click the E-Mail button, QuickBooks displays a drop-down list of commands that lets you e-mail either an Excel workbook or a PDF version of the report to someone else. When you choose one of the commands that says you want to e-mail a report, what QuickBooks does depends on whether QuickBooks sees that you have an e-mail program already set up and installed. If QuickBooks doesn't see any such program, QuickBooks displays the Edit E-Mail Information dialog box. If QuickBooks does see such a program, QuickBooks starts the e-mail program and adds the report as an attachment to a new message.

Exporting

If you click the Excel button, QuickBooks displays the Send Report to Excel dialog box (see Figure 6-6). You can use this dialog box to create an Excel report that holds the same information as shown in the report. (To do this, just select the Create New Worksheet radio button in the Send Report to Excel dialog box and then click the Export button.) You can also get fancier in your exporting by exporting a comma-separated values (CSV) file (these files can be opened by other electronic spreadsheet programs and by database programs), by exporting to a specific Excel workbook file, and by clicking the Advanced button to display another dialog box that lets you control how the exported information is formatted.

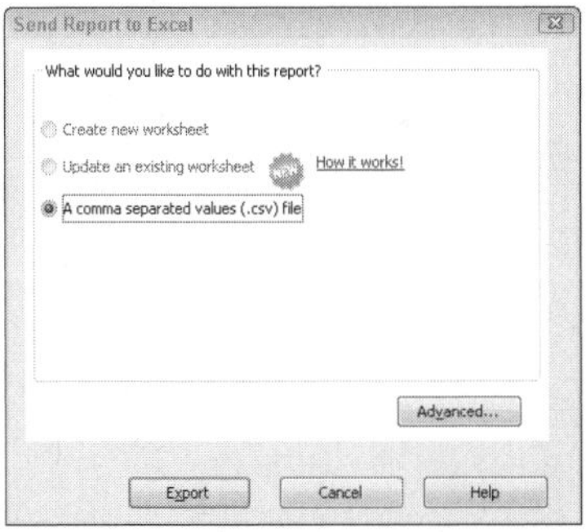

Figure 6-6: The Send Report to Excel dialog box.

A friendly suggestion, perhaps? Feel free to experiment with all the special exporting options. Just remember that after you export a QuickBooks report to a new, blank Excel workbook, you can also do any of this fancy-dancey stuff — special formatting and so on — there.

The other buttons and boxes

If you want to see how the Hide Header, Collapse, and Dates stuff works, just noodle around. You can't hurt anything.

If you change the report dates, click the Refresh button to update the report. To set refresh options for reports, choose Edit➪Preferences. Then click the Reports & Graphs icon in the list on the left and click the My Preferences tab if necessary. Click one of the Reports and Graphs options and then click OK.

Reports Made to Order

If you intend to print a large number of reports — and, more important, if you intend to print a large number of reports and show them to customers, investors, and other significant people — you want your reports to look good and to be easy to understand. I believe that beauty is in the eye of the beholder, so I'm not going to get into the aesthetics of report layouts. What I am going to do is explain how you can make QuickBooks reports look exactly the way you want them to look.

Choose Edit⇨Preferences. Click the Reports & Graphs icon in the list on the left and then click the Company Preferences tab to see the Preferences dialog box, as shown in Figure 6-7, for reports and graphs.

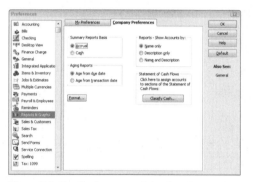

Figure 6-7: The Preferences dialog box for reports and graphs.

Here are your options:

✔ **Accrual:** *Accrual* is one of those cruel accounting terms that are hard to understand at first. If you select the Accrual radio button in the Summary Reports Basis panel, you tell QuickBooks to include all your transactions, sales, purchases, expenses, and so on, from the moment they're recorded, not from the time you receive or pay cash for them.

Accountants follow the accrual method because it gives a more accurate picture of profits. Also, the Internal Revenue Service (IRS) says that big corporations must use accrual accounting for their tax returns.

✔ **Cash:** If you select the Cash radio button, all the financial transactions in your reports are counted at the time you make your expense payments and you receive your customers' payments.

✔ **Age from Due Date:** If you select the Age from Due Date radio button in the Aging Reports panel, QuickBooks counts your expenses and invoices from the day that they fall due. Otherwise, QuickBooks counts them from the day they're recorded.

✔ **Format:** Click the Format button if you want to improve the look of your reports. In the Report Format Preferences dialog box that appears, as shown in Figure 6-8, you can use the Header/Footer tab to choose preferences for displaying the company name, the report title, the subtitle, and so on.

✔ **Reports – Show Accounts By:** You select a radio button in the Reports – Show Accounts By button group to indicate how you want QuickBooks to arrange account information on your reports: by name, by description, or by both name and description.

✔ **Statement of Cash Flows:** You click the Classify Cash button to tell QuickBooks how it should handle its accounts when it produces a picture-perfect statement of cash flows using generally accepted accounting principles. A suggestion? Leave this for your CPA.

You can use the Fonts & Numbers tab in the Report Format Preferences dialog box to choose preferences for displaying numbers, decimal fractions, and negative numbers. You also can fool around with different fonts and point sizes for labels, column headings, titles, and other things in your reports.

Click the Revert button in the Report Format Preferences dialog box to undo your customization changes.

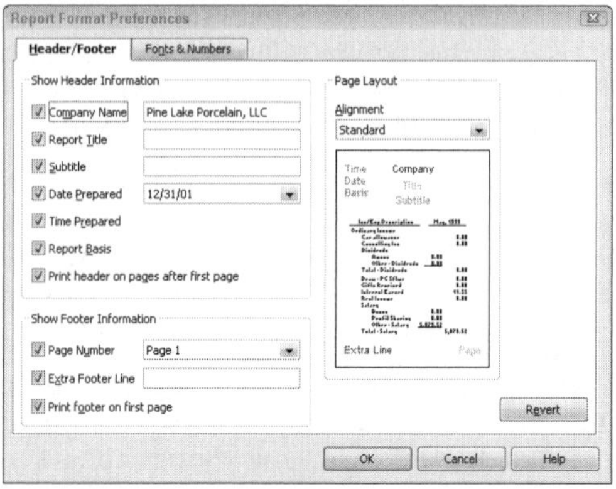

Figure 6-8: The Report Format Preferences dialog box.

Processing Multiple Reports

Want to print several reports at once? No problem. Choose Reports⇨Process Multiple Reports. When QuickBooks displays the Process Multiple Reports dialog box, as shown in Figure 6-9, select the reports that you want to print or display.

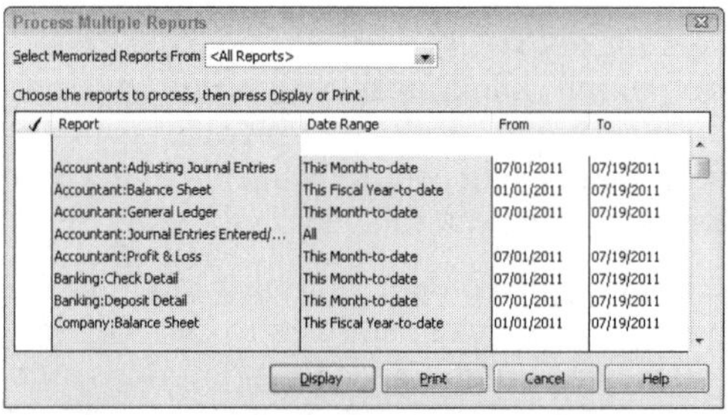

Figure 6-9: The Process Multiple Reports dialog box.

Your Other Reporting Options

Some versions of QuickBooks present you with a handful of additional report menu commands. These additional report menu commands are especially numerous in the Enterprise Solutions version of QuickBooks. I'm going to just ever so briefly touch upon some of these commands:

✓ **Custom Reports:** Displays commands you can use to create reports from scratch, following your specific instructions. These custom reports are pretty easy to use if you've noodled around much with the report customization options I mention earlier in the chapter.

✓ **Company Snapshot:** Displays a window with a bunch of little graphs and tables that summarize various snidbits of financial data: trends in income and expense, big account balances, open invoices, and so forth.

✓ **QuickBooks Statement Writer:** Starts the Intuit Statement Writer add-on program that will create financial statements using Microsoft Excel. Intuit Statement Writer comes with the Enterprise Solutions version of QuickBooks but is available in other versions of QuickBooks, too.

✓ **Combine Reports from Multiple Companies:** Allows you to create a consolidated report using data from more than one QuickBooks company file. When you choose the command, QuickBooks displays a dialog box that you use to identity the company files and the report combination you want.

Last but Not Least: The QuickReport

The QuickReport is one of the best kinds of reports, so I saved it for last. You can generate a QuickReport from a list, from invoices and bills with names of people or items on them, and from account registers. QuickReports are especially useful when you're studying a list and see something that momentarily baffles you. Simply make sure that the item you're curious about is highlighted, click the Reports button, and choose the QuickReports command for the item from the drop-down list.

You can also right-click an item and choose QuickReport from the shortcut menu to create a QuickReport of the item.

Figure 6-10 shows a QuickReport produced from a register. I clicked the QuickReport button to display this Register QuickReport window with the transaction information for a vendor: the fictitious Big Bertha's Workshop.

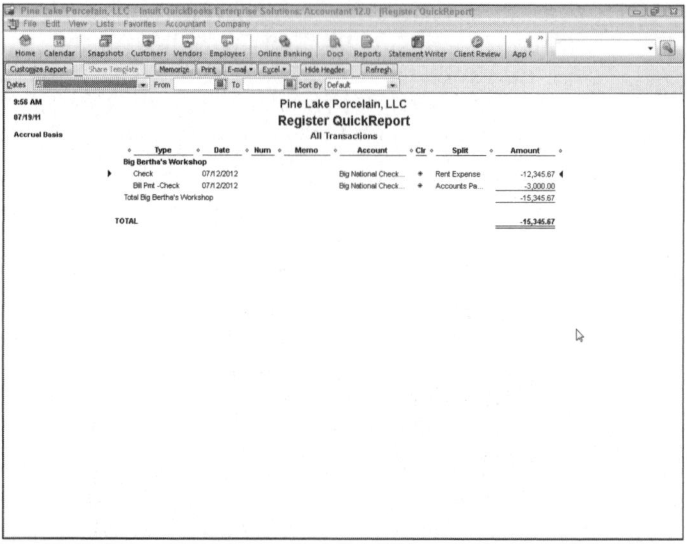

Figure 6-10: A QuickReport report.

The QuickReport option is also on the Reports menu when you have a register or list open. Often times, then, you can display a QuickReport from a form — even though no QuickReport button appears — by choosing the menu option. For example, if you're writing a check to a vendor, you can enter the company's name on the check and choose Reports⊏>QuickReport to see a report of transactions involving the company.

Chapter 7

(Almost) Ten Tips for Business Owners

● ●

In This Chapter

▶ Supply your own signature

▶ Don't sign a check with a scrawl

▶ Look over canceled checks before your bookkeeper does

▶ Select a QuickBooks bookkeeper

▶ Regularly review your financial statements

▶ Understand that cash-basis accounting doesn't work for all businesses

▶ Know what to do if QuickBooks doesn't work for your business

▶ Keep things simple

● ●

*I*f you run a business and you use QuickBooks, you need to know the information in this chapter. You can get this information by sitting down with your certified public accountant (CPA) over a cup of coffee at $200 per hour. Or, you can read this chapter.

Sign All Your Own Checks

I have nothing against your bookkeeper. In a small business, however, people — especially full-charge bookkeepers — can bamboozle you too darn easily. By signing all the checks yourself, you keep your fingers on the pulse of your cash outflow.

Yeah, I know this practice can be a hassle. I know that you can't easily spend three months in Hawaii. I know that you have to wade through paperwork every time you sign a stack of checks.

By the way, if you're in a partnership, I think that you should have at least a couple of the partners co-sign checks.

Don't Sign a Check the Wrong Way

If you sign many checks, you may be tempted to use a John Hancock–like signature. Although scrawling your name illegibly makes great sense when you're autographing baseballs, don't do it when you're signing checks. A clear signature, especially one with a sense of personal style, is distinctive. A wavy line with a cross and a couple of dots is easy to forge.

Which leads me to my next tip. . . .

Review Canceled Checks Before Your Bookkeeper Does

Be sure that you review your canceled checks before anybody else sees the monthly bank statement.

This chapter isn't about browbeating bookkeepers. Still, a business owner can determine whether someone is forging signatures on checks only by being the first to open the bank statement and by reviewing each of the canceled-check signatures.

If you don't examine the checks, unscrupulous employees — especially bookkeepers who can update the bank account records — can forge your signature with impunity. And they won't get caught if they never overdraw the account.

I won't continue this rant, but let me mention one last thing: Every time I teach CPAs about how to better help their clients with QuickBooks, I hear again and again about business owners who haven't been careful about keeping an eye on the bookkeeper — and have suffered embezzlement and forgery as a result.

If you don't follow these procedures, you — not the bank — will probably eat the losses.

Choose a Bookkeeper Who Is Familiar with Computers and Knows How to Do Payroll

Don't worry. You don't need to request an FBI background check.

In fact, if you use QuickBooks, you don't need to hire people who are familiar with small business accounting systems. Just find people who know how to keep a checkbook and work with a computer. They shouldn't have a problem understanding QuickBooks.

Of course, you don't want someone who just fell off the turnip truck. But even if you do hire someone who rode into town on one, you're not going to have much trouble getting that person up-to-speed with QuickBooks.

A bookkeeper who knows double-entry bookkeeping is super-helpful. But to be fair, such knowledge probably isn't essential. I will say this, however: When you're hiring, find someone who knows how to do payroll — and not just the federal payroll tax stuff, but also the state payroll tax monkey business.

Regularly Review Your Financial Statements

Truly, truly, I'm not trying to increase the headache factor of your running your small business. The whole purpose of this book is to make your small business's accounting flow more smoothly. But nevertheless I want to add a task to your to-do list: You need to regularly review your financial statements.

In other words, regularly produce and look over the profit and loss statement that QuickBooks effortlessly generates. Get habitual about looking over your balance sheet with its lists of assets and liabilities. Explore and find another report or two that gives you useful insights into the rhythms and rhymes of your business. (Any errors you make will probably show up as goofy numbers on your balance sheet, by the way.)

Probably, you can keep a pretty firm handle on the operation by looking at two or three easy-to-understand reports. And by regularly peeking at these financial statements — say a time or two a week — you turn your accounting system into a tool useful both for spotting tempting opportunities and for avoiding dangerous traps.

No kidding, I run my businesses by looking at three QuickBooks reports: a profit and loss statement that compares the current year's and previous year's year-to-date numbers (so I can see how I'm doing in the current year as compared to the previous year), the accounts receivable summary aging (so I can see which clients and customers are past due), and the balance sheet (so I can monitor my cash and working capital and spot any funny stuff).

Choose an Appropriate Accounting System

When you use QuickBooks, you use either cash-basis accounting or accrual-basis accounting.

Cash-basis accounting is fine when a business' cash inflow mirrors its sales and its cash outflow mirrors its expenses. This situation isn't the case, however, in many businesses. A contractor of single-family homes, for example, may have cash coming in (by borrowing from banks) but may not make any money. Alternatively, a pawnshop owner who lends money at 22 percent might make scads of money, even if cash pours out of the business daily.

As a general rule, when you're buying and selling inventory, accrual-basis accounting works better than cash-basis accounting. However, cash-basis accounting typically defers income taxes.

If QuickBooks Doesn't Work for Your Business

QuickBooks is a great small business accounting program. In fact, I'd even go as far as to say that QuickBooks is probably the best small business accounting program available.

However, if QuickBooks doesn't seem to fit your needs — if, for example, you need a program that works better for a manufacturer or that includes some special industry-specific feature — you may want one of the more complicated (but also more powerful) small business accounting packages.

Be sure before you jump from QuickBooks Simple Start or QuickBooks Pro to check out the Enterprise Solutions version of QuickBooks, which costs more but also works for bigger businesses. The Enterprise version of QuickBooks looks and works almost identically to the "regular" versions of QuickBooks. If you know QuickBooks Pro, accordingly, you already know (or mostly know) QuickBooks Enterprise.

If the Enterprise version of QuickBooks doesn't work, you may want to talk to your accountant about industry-specific packages. (For example, if you're a commercial printer, some vendor may have developed a special accounting package just for commercial printers.)

I'm amazed that PC accounting software remains so affordable. You can buy a great accounting package — one that you can use to manage a $5 million or a $25 million business — for a few hundred bucks. Accounting software is truly one of the great bargains in life.

Keep Things Simple

Let me share one last comment about managing small business financial affairs: Keep things as simple as possible. In fact, keep your business affairs simple enough that you can easily tell whether you're making money and whether the business is healthy.

This advice may sound strange, but as a CPA, I've worked for some very bright people who have built monstrously complex financial structures for their businesses, including complicated leasing arrangements, labyrinthine partnership and corporate structures, and sophisticated profit-sharing and cost-sharing arrangements with other businesses.

I can offer only anecdotal evidence, of course, but I strongly believe that these super-sophisticated financial arrangements don't produce a profit when you consider all the costs. What's more, these super-sophisticated arrangements almost always turn into management and record-keeping headaches.

Of course, the one positive thing you can say about such arrangements is this: You'll make both your accountant and lawyer happy. And rich. So that's good for them, at least.

Index

• A •

Account Not Found box, 73, 140, 148
accountant and taxes reports, 159
accounting system, 6–7, 176–177
accounts payable method (A/P),
    131, 141
Accounts Payable register window,
    147, 154
accrual, 168
accrual-basis accounting, 25, 56,
    132, 176
accumulated depreciation, 11
agings, 124
A/P (accounts payable method),
    131, 141
ASCII text file, 163
Assess Finance Charges window, 127

• B •

bank deposits, 119–123
banking reports, 159
Banks Accounts dialog box, 24
Billing Rate Levels list, 58–59
bills
    Billing Rate Levels list, 58–59
    deletion of, 148–149
    electronic banking and billing, 9
    Enter Bills window, 142
    how paid bill looks in register, 153
    Pay Bills window, 151
    payment of, 131–132, 143,
        149–154
    recording of, 141–149
bookkeepers, 173–175
budgets and forecasts reports, 160
Business Contact Information
    dialog box, 21

• C •

cash inflow, ways to improve,
    123–129
cash-basis accounting, 132, 176
chart of accounts
    adding accounts to, 73
    based on industry, 18
    description of, 18–19, 65
    finalizing of, 65
    as list, 65
Chart of Accounts window, 68
cheat sheet, 105, 116, 122, 151
Check Register window, 140
checks
    forms for, 138
    reviewing canceled checks,
        174–175
    sample of completed check, 136
    signatures on, 173–174
    writing of, 132–141
Circular E (IRS), 44
Class list, 59–60
classes, 59
COGS (Cost of Goods Sold), 36
coinage, 120
comma delimited file, 163
comma-separated values (CSV)
    file, 167
company and financial reports, 158
Computer Associates, 11
conversion date, 9
Cost of Goods Sold (COGS), 36
Create Credit Memos/Refunds
    window
    completed, 89
    empty, 86

Create Invoices window
  completed, 83
  empty, 77
Create New Design web page, 100
credit memos
  Create Credit Memos/Refunds
    window, completed, 89
  Create Credit Memos/Refunds
    window, empty, 86
  customization of, 100–101
  fixing mistakes on, 90
  forms for, 91
  preparation of, 86–90
  printing of, 91–99
  sending of, via e-mail, 99–100
creditors, 11
CSV (comma-separated values)
  file, 167
Customer Center window, 123
customer deposits, 128–129
customer history information,
  90–91
Customer Invoices window, 91
Customer Message list, 61
customer payments, 114–119
customer receivables, 25, 158
Customer Types list, 60–61
customers
  adding of, to customer list, 45–48
  Additional Info tab, 47
  Customer Center window, 123
  deposits of, 128–129
  history information, 90–91
  Job Info tab, 51
  messages for, 57, 61, 82, 88, 108
  New Customer window, 45–48
  Payment Info tab, 47
  payments by, 114–119
  receivables, 25, 158
  reports, 158
  setting up jobs for, 48–52
  types of, 60–61

• D •

destination point, 81
Discount and Credits dialog box, 117
Discount item type, 39, 40–41
discounts, itemizing of
  on invoices, 38, 40, 82, 88, 118
  on receipts, 107
double-checking, 73–74

• E •

electronic banking and billing, 9
e-mail
  for reports, 166
  for sending invoices and credit
    memos, 99–100
employees
  adding of, to employee list, 42–44
  New Employee window, 43–44
  reports, 159
Enter Bills window, 142
Enter Sales Receipts window
  completed, 109
  empty, 104
Enterprise Solutions versions, 1, 2,
  15, 16, 36, 170, 171, 177
Excel, 20, 163, 164, 166, 167, 171
express setup, 17–24

• F •

finance charges, assessment of,
  124–128
financial reports, 158
financial statements
  created by Intuit Statement
    Writer, 171
  review of, 175–176
Fine Alignment dialog box, 93
Fixed Asset list, 57–58

fixed assets, 57
Fixed Assets Item List window, 58
FOB (free-on-board), 80
forecasts reports, 160
forms
  for credit memos, 91
  Customize Your QuickBooks Forms window, 100, 101, 105
  Intuit Preprinted Forms, 93, 95, 97, 110
  for invoices, 91, 92
  for payroll taxes, 43
  for preprinted checks, 138
  1099s, 55
  as timesavers, 8
  W-2 statements, 14, 44
free-on-board (FOB), 80

• *G* •

general journal entries
  Make General Journal Entries window, completed, 73
  Make General Journal Entries window, empty, 72
Group item type, 31, 39–40
group items, 40–41

• *I* •

icons, explained, 3–4
income statement, 161
industry-specific features, need for, 177
industry-specific reports, 160
Internal Revenue Service. *See* IRS
Intuit Preprinted Forms, 93, 95, 97, 110
Intuit Quicken, 11
Intuit Statement Writer, 171
Intuit web page, 97

inventory
  accrual-basis accounting compared to cash-basis accounting for, 177
  adding a new item to, 38
  items returned to, 88
  needed for setup, 14
  reports, 159
  tracked and nontracked, 22
  using reminders for reordering of, 35, 36, 63
Inventory Assembly item type, 31, 35–37
Inventory Part item type, 31, 33–35
invoice forms, 91, 92
invoice printer, 92
invoices
  Customer Invoices window, 91
  customization of, 100–101
  deletion of, 85–86
  fixing mistakes on, 84–85
  forms for, 91, 92
  preparation of, 76–84
  printing of, 91–98
  sample, 29
  sending of, via e-mail, 99–100
  types of, 76
IRS (Internal Revenue Service)
  Circular E, 44
  requirements of, 8, 169
  rules for deducting business miles, 155
  1099 contractor, 55
  1099 form, 55
  W-2 statements, 14, 44
Item list, 27
Item List window, 30
item types
  Discount, 39, 40–41
  Group, 31, 39–40
  Inventory Assembly, 31, 35–37
  Inventory Part, 31, 33–35
  Payment, 32, 37–38

Sales Tax, 32, 37, 41
Service, 31, 33
Subtotal, 31, 38–39
item(s)
  defined, 28
  editing of, 41–42
  New Item window, 30, 34, 39, 42
  types of, 31–32

• *J* •

Job Types list, 60–61
jobs
  New Job window, 49–52
  reports, 159

• *L* •

Layout Designer window, 101
list reports, 160
lists
  exporting items to word
    processor, 64–65
  organizing of, 63–64
  printing of, 64
  types of, 57

• *M* •

Make General Journal Entries
    window
  completed, 73
  empty, 72
Make Payments window, 121
manufacturers, accounting needs
    of, 177
Memorize Report dialog box, 166
Memorized Transaction list, 63
merchant fees, 116, 123
messages
  on checks, 135
  for customers, 57, 61, 82, 88, 108

Microsoft Excel, 20, 163, 164, 166,
    167, 171
mileage
  reports, 159
  tracking of, 154–155
mistakes, fixing of
  on credit memos, 90
  on entries for customer
    payments, 119
  on invoices, 84–85
  on sales receipts, 113–114
Modify Report dialog box, 165

• *N* •

Name Not Found box, 134, 139
New Customer window, 45–48
New Employee window, 43–44
New Item window
  empty, 30
  with Inventory Part item type
    selected, 34
  with item type Group selected, 39
  for item type Sales Tax Group, 42
New Job window, 49–52
Non-Inventory Part type, 31, 33
not found boxes
  Account Not Found box, 73, 140, 148
  Name Not Found box, 134, 139
  Vendor Not Found box, 147

• *O* •

Opening Balance Equity register, 70
Other Charge type, 31, 33
Other Names list, 60

• *P* •

Pay Bills window, 151
Pay Sales Tax dialog box, 156

payables reports, 159
Payment item type, 32, 37–38
Payment Method list, 62
payments
 fixing mistakes on entries for, 119
 Make Payments window, 121
 Payments to Deposit dialog
  box, 121
 Receive Payments window, 115
 recording of, 114–119
Payments to Deposit dialog box, 121
payroll reports, 159
People You Do Business With
 dialog box, 22
PO (purchase order), 144
Preferences dialog box
 for finance charges, 125
 for reminders, 150
 for reports and graphs, 168
Price Level list, 58
Print Invoices dialog box, 97
Print One Invoice dialog box, 95
Print One Sales Receipt dialog
 box, 110
Print Reports dialog box, 163
Printer Setup dialog box, 92
Process Multiple Reports dialog
 box, 170
product credit memo, 86
product invoice, 76
Products and Services You Sell
 dialog box, 23
professional (service) credit
 memo, 86
professional (service) invoice, 76
profit and loss report
 creating a standard version, 161
 description of, 158
 sample, 8, 162
purchase order (PO), 144
purchases reports, 159

• Q •

QuickBooks 2011 For Dummies
 (Rathbone), 4
QuickBooks Enterprise, 1, 2, 15, 16,
 36, 170, 171, 177
QuickBooks Point of Sales
 system, 112
QuickBooks Premier, 1, 2
QuickBooks Pro, 1, 2, 15, 16, 36, 177
QuickBooks Simple Start, 1, 2, 13,
 15, 177
QuickBooks Simple Start For
 Dummies (Rathbone), 15
Quicken, 11
QuickReports, 157, 171–172
QuickZoom, 164

• R •

Rathbone, Andy (author), 5
 QuickBooks Simple Start For
  Dummies, 15
 QuickBooks 2011 For Dummies, 4
 Windows For Dummies, 5
receivables reports, 158
Receive Payments window, 115
refunds, 86, 89
register
 Accounts Payable register
  window, 147, 154
 Check Register window, 140
 defined, 68
 how paid bill looks in, 153
 Opening Balance Equity
  register, 70
Reminders list, 35, 36, 63, 149–150
Report Center window, 161

reports
  categories of, 158–160
  creating and printing of, 161–164
  editing and rearranging of, 164–166
  e-mailing of, 166
  exporting of, 167
  made to order, 168–170
  other options for, 170–171
  processing of multiple, 170
  QuickReports, 171–172
  QuickZoom feature, 164
retailers, special tips for, 111–112

• S •

sales receipts
  Enter Sales Receipts window, completed, 109
  Enter Sales Receipts window, empty, 104
  fixing mistakes on, 113–114
  printing of, 109–111
  recording of, 104–109
Sales Rep list, 60
sales reports, 158
sales tax, payment of, 155–156
Sales Tax Code list, 59
Sales Tax item type, 32, 37, 41
Select Invoices to Print dialog box, 96
Send Invoice dialog box, 99
Send Report to Excel dialog box, 167
service (professional) credit memo, 86
service (professional) invoice, 76
Service item type, 31, 33
setup, 15–24
Ship Via list, 62
shipping point, 80
simplicity, value of, 178
Simply Accounting, 11
subitems, 32

Subtotal item type, 31, 38–39
suspense accounts, 66

• T •

tab delimited file, 163
taxes reports, 159
Tell Us about Your Business dialog box, 18
templates, 165–166
1099 contractor, 55
1099 form, 55
Terms list, 61
time reports, 159
trial balance
  defined, 10–11
  sample, 12–13, 67, 71

• V •

Vehicle list, 62
vehicle mileage, tracking of, 154–155
Vendor Not Found box, 147
vendor payables, 25, 159
Vendor Types list, 60–61
vendors
  adding of, to vendor list, 52–57
  Additional Info tab, 54
  Address Info tab, 53
  payables, 25, 159
  reports, 159
  types of, 60–61

• W •

Windows For Dummies (Rathbone), 5
Write Checks window, 133

• Y •

You've Got a Company File! dialog box, 21